BEACHES, BERRIES and BLISS

BLUEBERRY RECIPES AND MORE

Tiffany Balk

Beaches, Berries & Bliss

Blueberry Recipes and More

Tiffany Balk

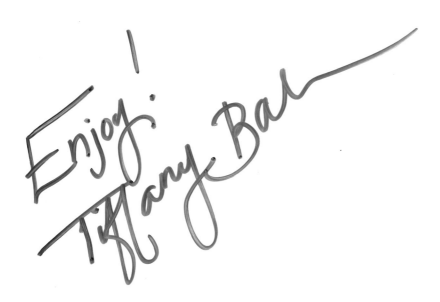

Enjoy!
Tiffany Balk

Beaches, Berries & Bliss

Blueberry Recipes and More

Published by

splatteredinkpress.com

ISBN: 978-1-939294-19-7

Dedication

For all my boys -
My husband, Steve,
And sons Keegan, Campbell and Cayce

Acknowledgments

It is crazy how life takes you through different turns, and writing this cookbook was one. Twenty years ago, I would have laughed at the idea of writing a cookbook, yet here it is.

This story would not have been possible without a lot of people. To my 'original family' of Mom and Dad (Pam and Giff Brown), my sister Katie (Brown) Rose and my little brother, Giff Brown - thank you for a great, fun and adventurous childhood.

Thank you to the Hazleton family (Dick, Mary Lou, Mary Jane, Chris, Steve and Greg) for contributing to my childhood with care and wonderful memories. Thank you to the Dow Corning Corporation for sending us on amazing adventures all over the world.

To my Blueberry Haven employees, Cheryl Grove and Pat Hoekman, thank you for your endless patience while we made the recipes to photograph, as well as for the recipes you added to make the cookbook even better. Thank you to Chris Parker for his willingness to test all my recipes so my handwritten notes made sense.

Thank you to my writing coach and publisher, Tricia L. McDonald, for keeping me on track, providing encouragement, and laughing as I shared my stories. Thank you to my editor, Barb Rickard, for her attention to detail and accuracy, and making me sound likeable at all times.

And especially, thank you to my husband Steve and my boys. They were always supportive as I wrote my 'story' and the cookbook, and were willing to taste my many recipes - the failed ones, as well as the good ones. Their patience while I became engulfed in the process was instrumental in my completing this journey.

Thank you to Keegan for listening to my ideas and dining solo with me on vacation. To Cayce for helping with the many photo shoots, and to Campbell and Ian for eating all the desserts after school.

Thanks most to Steve for always supporting my ideas, and encouraging me to act on them…even if he thought I was crazy.

Love you all-
Tiffany

Contents

Nana

Born in Lincoln, Maine, a small town about 45 minutes north of Bangor, I am the oldest of three children. For my first couple of years, I spent a lot of time with Nana, my maternal grandmother, so it is no surprise my earliest childhood memories are of helping in her kitchen.

Lincoln is located in northern Maine, and the town's survival depended on the paper mill, where many of the town residents were employed. The smell of the mill was a part of the town, and once you have smelled a paper mill you never forget the specific smell of stale vinegar, chemicals and smoke. Many people who lived in Lincoln called it Stinking Lincoln.

Nana and Papa lived on William Street, a little out of town where the stench of the mill wasn't so strong. Their yellow ranch house was on a hill with a huge weeping willow in the front yard. I often used the tree as my fort and had very elaborate home and tea parties set up underneath the branches.

Inside Nana and Papa's house, Nana had a very large and very pink kitchen. Maybe it was because I was a small child at the time, but I remember the kitchen as being huge. The cupboards and countertops were endless, and I loved opening and closing all the many cupboard doors. Some were so big I would crawl inside and play with Nana's many pots and pans. I also loved to stack her canned goods as tall as I could until they tipped over. I think Nana loved that the cans kept me entertained so she could keep moving with her daily chores, as she always let me stack away.

The floor was chocolate brown linoleum flecked with white and reminded me of Hershey© Kisses. The kitchen aroma was a strong coffee scent, and I believe Nana had a pot going all the time. My grandfather worked third shift at the paper mill, so strong coffee was always needed.

I helped Nana a lot in the kitchen when I was a young girl and remember helping her roll out dough for pie crust. Nana would pull up a pink vinyl and metal chair from the kitchen table to the counter for me to stand on. She always turned it around with the back of the chair against the cupboards, "so ya don't fall oveah," she would say. I would get up on the chair so I could reach the counter and be the same height as Nana. She was just a tiny little lady and only stood about five feet tall, with brown curly hair and big brown eyes.

Nana would sprinkle flour on the counter top and hand me the wooden rolling pin. I would do my best to roll out the dough so it would cover the entire pie plate. The whole time I would be rolling, Nana would be chatting away, encouraging me to just keep rolling. Nana was busy, always in constant motion, moving, walking and talking very fast.

"Keep rolling," she would say. "You almost have the crust rolled out so it will be the perfect size for the blueberry pie."

I loved blueberry pie, especially Nana's as she made the best buttery tasting pie crust. Nana's blueberry pie had very few ingredients besides blueberries, because she said that was all it needed since blueberries were sweet enough. She didn't even follow a recipe but would put the blueberries in the pie shell until it was full, sprinkle the blueberries with sugar and squeeze half of a lemon on top of the sugar-coated blueberries. Then she would top with another buttery crust.

"No pie till aftah suppah," she would say in her thick Maine accent as we took the perfect golden pie out of the oven to cool.

NANA'S BLUEBERRY PIE

LOBSTER SALAD with BLUEBERRIES

Nana's Blueberry Pie

Serves 6

For filling:
4 or more cups of blueberries
4 tablespoons sugar
Squeeze of lemon juice

For crust:
3 cups flour
⅛ teaspoon salt
1¾ sticks very cold unsalted butter, cut into tiny pieces
1 large egg
6 tablespoons ice water

Preheat oven to 350°.

In a large bowl, combine flour and salt; add butter and mix together well with a pastry cutter or your fingers. In a small bowl, mix together the water and egg. Combine this with the butter mixture until it is all mixed together. Cut the dough in half and wrap in Saran© wrap. Place in the refrigerator and allow to chill for at least one hour. After an hour, lightly flour the counter and roll out the dough.

For pie filling:
Place the first rolled out crust into the pie plate. Add the fresh blueberries, sprinkle with sugar and the fresh lemon juice. Top with the other rolled out crust. Bake for an hour at 350°.

Lobster Salad with Blueberries

Serves 4

2 whole lobsters, cooked, cleaned and cut into pieces
Salt and pepper to taste
Olive oil to drizzle
3 stalks celery, finely diced
2 ears fresh corn
¼ medium red onion, finely diced
1½ cups blueberries
3 tablespoons fresh dill, minced
4 tablespoons mayo
4 tablespoons sour cream
¼ cup half and half
1 whole lemon
1 teaspoon sugar
¼ cup crumbled feta cheese

With a very sharp knife, shave off each corn cob into a large
bowl. Combine with the onion and celery, and set aside.

For dressing: Mix together mayo, sour cream, feta, and half
and half. Stir in sugar, juice from lemon, salt and pepper.
Taste a small amount and add more salt, if necessary.

Put the lobster meat in the bowl with celery, onion and
corn. Stir to combine. Pour half the dressing over the
ingredients and toss lightly, adding more dressing if
needed. Don't add too much, as it should be lightly coated.
Toss in the blueberries and mix carefully. Sprinkle on feta
cheese. Serve over lettuce or as a lobster roll on your
favorite bun.

Down to Camp

Summer time for many people who lived in Lincoln, Maine, was spent "down to camp," as Nana said. Down to camp actually meant living at the lake for the summer. I suppose it was called "down," because Cold Stream Pond was in Enfield, Maine, about 12 miles south of Lincoln. There was no paper mill smell there, just the lush scent of the great outdoors. If you were from Maine, you knew the outdoors was full of pine trees. My favorite scent still today is of wet pine trees, just like the smell of down to camp.

Cold Stream Pond was not a pond but a crystal clear, spring-fed lake that was freezing cold. It was seven miles long and many miles across in some areas. In the quiet of the morning, you could often hear loons.

The camp we stayed at on Cold Stream was known as the Neeland Camp. It was a small summer house on the shores of the Cold Stream Pond. We spent six weeks at this camp every summer until I was about 16 years old, and it is my version of roughing it. There was no running fresh water or hot water at the camp. It came right from the lake, and we had to boil it for washing dishes. We had to walk with our wagon full of empty milk jugs for water and fill them from the fresh

water spring. I thought the spring was miles away because it took forever to get there, but it was really less than half a mile away. However, at such a young age, walking down a dirt road pulling a wagon full of water jugs, it seemed like it was forever from the camp.

Roughing it was also having only one toilet, and it was not a true bathroom -- it was a flushing toilet in its own little building on the backside of the camp. I was glad it wasn't an outhouse with just a hole in the ground, and at least we had 'a pot.' Lucky for us the bathroom only smelled like a wooden hut, instead of the smell that came with an outhouse.

At night if you had to go to the bathroom, you had to go outside to the toilet. I usually woke up my sister, cousin, or Nana to go with me if I got up in the middle of the night. I was always petrified there was going to be a moose or a bear outside as I had seen a moose once when I was walking to the spring to get water. I nearly had a heart attack when I looked up from getting water and there stood this HUGE animal -- and it wasn't a deer. I ran as fast as I could back to camp and explained to Nana what I had seen.

"Just a moose," she said.

The camp had few rooms: a kitchen, living area, and on the lakeside of the camp, a large screened-in porch filled with painted red and white rocking chairs. We had no television at the camp, so I spent many hours on the porch reading and playing board games. Nana was the best at Yahtzee©. She threw more yahtzees than anyone I knew.

The camp had an upstairs where we all slept: my mom and dad, my sister, my brother, Nana and I. Papa had to sleep downstairs in the bed under the stairs because he snored so loudly. Upstairs was one big room, divided by three walls, making it seem like four separate bedrooms. Mom and Dad slept in a queen bed covered with a white chenille flowered bedspread. Their room was on the left side of the big room that faced the lake. There was a dividing wall that didn't go all the way to the ceiling, with a space from the wall to the ceiling. This space was large enough so we could throw pillows or other objects at the person who slept in the queen bed with the pink chenille bedspread on the right side of the room facing the lake. Mostly Nana slept there, but sometimes Nana and Papa went back to their big house in Lincoln to stay. That was when our other aunts and uncles came down to camp. There were many pillows tossed back and forth between those walls, with lots of laughter, too.

My bed was in the room on the right that faced the road, but I was only about five feet from Nana's bed. Katie, who was 4, was in the room in front of my mom and dad's bed, along with Giffie's crib.

There were many mornings when I was awakened by the aroma of pancakes. Katie and I loved having Nana cook us breakfast, and we would run down the rickety camp steps to find Nana hustling around the kitchen fixing breakfast.

Usually Giffie was already strapped in his high chair placed in the middle of the kitchen so he couldn't get into everything while Nana was cooking. The kitchen at the camp had cupboards with no doors, so the contents of the cupboards were only covered with white curtains, decorated with red, blue and yellow sailboats. This made it easy for Giffie to get into all the glass plates and glasses in the cupboards. Nana worried Giffie would hurt himself which is why she would pop him in his highchair in the middle of the room.

Nana was always waiting for me and Katie as we ran into the kitchen in the morning.

"You girls want some pan-ie cakes?" she would ask.

We couldn't wait to have some of her special lemon pancakes. They were always perfectly golden, never too thin or too thick. She also made homemade blueberry syrup that was delicious. Giffie usually had syrup all over himself and the stainless steel tray of his high chair. Papa would be sitting at the kitchen table, reading the newspaper with his cup of coffee.

Nana got our breakfast ready as mom and dad had gotten up earlier and gone into town to get groceries and do laundry at the laundromat. That was their time to escape the hustle and bustle of camp living.

As soon as they returned, we would be bugging them to take us waterskiing, fishing, boating or hiking.

Being down at camp was always a fun, yet relaxing time, and summers seemed to last forever. There was always an endless amount to do, and it was fun having my many cousins, aunts, uncles and grandparents staying under one roof.

LEMON BLUEBERRY PANCAKES

BLUEBERRY SYRUP

Lemon Blueberry Pancakes

Serves 6

1 lemon
1 cup milk
1¼ cup flour
Pinch of salt
½ teaspoon baking soda
2 tablespoons of sugar
1 egg
2 tablespoons butter, melted
¾ cup fresh blueberries (if in season) or ¾ cup Blueberry Haven Dried Blueberries

Zest one lemon and squeeze lemon to get about 2 teaspoons worth of lemon juice. Add the 2 teaspoons lemon juice into one cup of milk. In a medium bowl, combine flour, salt, soda, sugar and 1 teaspoon of lemon zest; mix together with a fork. Whisk egg in a bowl until frothy and pour into flour mixture. Add the melted butter and lemony milk to flour mixture, mixing all together. Fold in the blueberries.

Spray a large pan with cooking oil and heat over medium heat. Pour batter in about 1/3 cup measurements onto pan and cook on both sides until done.

Blueberry Syrup

Serves 6

4 cups blueberries
3 cups water
1 tablespoon lemon juice
1 cup Blueberry Haven Blossom Honey
¼ cup flour

In a small pot, add blueberries, honey and enough water to cover the berries. Bring to a boil, and then let the blueberries cool, approximately 3 minutes.

In another bowl, mix flour and 1 cup water until there are no lumps. Stir the flour mixture into the hot berry mixture and cook -- it should thicken nicely. Add the lemon juice, stir and serve. We like it hot or cold.

Moving to the Mitten State

In the early 70's, we moved from New England to the Midwest and settled into Midland, Michigan, a small town in the middle of the Mitten State. My dad had taken a job with Dow Corning Corporation, one of the largest silicon companies in the world. We moved to Michigan in the late summer and enjoyed our life in Midland, but once summer came, we were ready to see Nana, Papa and our cousins. So, in June our family took its annual trip to Lincoln to spend time at camp and the lake. Our route to Maine started by going through Michigan's thumb, traveling into Canada, going across New York, Massachusetts, and New Hampshire, and then landing in Maine. The drive from Michigan to Cold Stream Pond was about 18 hours.

We usually left in the early evening, which is why I think our parents dressed us in our pajamas, so we would think it was night time and sleep most of the way. Katie and I had matching summer nighties that were sleeveless and lavender. Giffie was always in his footie pajamas, whether it was hot or cold. Once we were all loaded in the car, away we would go on the long road trip.

Our car was a blue (not navy or royal blue, but an in-between blue) 1974 Ford Gran Torino. Cars were BIG in the 70's and the Ford seemed about the length of a football field. My dad, mom and Giffie were in the front. Katie (who was four) and I (who was eight) sat in the back seat. However, if Giffie was awake, which was about 17 hours of the 18-hour drive, he would hop between the front and back seats the whole drive. I always hoped that Katie wouldn't get car sick, but she did. I always had to go to the bathroom and wanted to stop all the time. My parents figured they could solve both the car sickness and the peeing problem by having a big Maxwell© House coffee can with a plastic lid on the floor in the front seat. When I complained about needing to go to the bathroom, I could use the coffee can to pee in. I always hoped that I had to pee before Katie was sick. I'm sure you can imagine the smell in the inside of the car when the lid came off.

Peeing in the coffee can became routine on our trips and made stopping much less frequent. We thought nothing of peeing in our own mini portable toilet as there was plenty of room between the dashboard and the seat for the coffee can. Giffie sometimes even sat on the blue car mats up in the front by Mom's feet, playing with cars.

At some point on the long drive, Katie and I would fall asleep, and when we woke up, we would be in Vacationland -- the state of Maine and Cold Stream Pond. After we were awake and had used the coffee can, Mom would pull out a thermos of milk for us and would hand us slices of blueberry banana bread packed in baggies. Our snack was to hold us over until we could stop for a real bathroom break.

My parents had a large thermos of coffee they drank the whole way to keep them awake and alert for the long drive, and to help them deal with Giffie.

We traveled to Maine every other summer for the first five years we lived in Michigan and used the coffee can every time we went.

MAM'S BLUEBERRY BANANA BREAD

BLUEBERRY ICED COFFEE

Mam's Blueberry Banana Bread

Serves 8

1 cup sugar
1 stick butter
2 eggs
3 ripe bananas
1¾ cups flour
1 teaspoon baking soda
½ teaspoon baking powder
1 cup Blueberry Haven Dried Blueberries

Preheat oven to 300°

Cream together sugar and butter; add eggs and mashed bananas, and mix well. In a separate bowl, mix flour, soda, and powder. Slowly mix the dry ingredients into the wet ingredients. Fold in the blueberries.

Bake at 300° in greased loaf pan for 70 minutes.

Blueberry Iced Coffee

Serves 6

1 **cup** Blueberry Haven Ground Blueberry Coffee

1 quart of cold water

Combine both ingredients in glass jar, cover and leave at room temperature for at least 10 hours.

When ready, pour all through a coffee filter into another container. Refrigerate and serve over ice.

Where is Brussels?

In 1976, I was in the fourth grade when my dad came home from work and announced that we were moving. We had recently moved from our first house on Adams Street to a house on Tyler Street, which was just around the corner. Being 10 years old, I thought we were just moving to another new house.

That night, we were all gathered around our brown walnut kitchen table for dinner. As usual, mom and dad sat at the heads of the table, Katie and I sat on the sides, and Giffie was in his high chair between me and Mom. Dad looked at my mom, smiled and explained in greater detail where we were moving.

"We are moving out of the United States to Brussels," he said.

"Where in Ohio is Brussels?" I asked.

He started laughing, but I didn't think it was funny. I had no clue where Brussels was, let alone Belgium, and who moved out of country? And besides, everyone in Michigan that I knew treated Ohio like it was in another country.

My parents acted like it was pretty normal to move wherever there was a good job and a better advancement for my father's career, so we knew we would be making the best of the situation whether we liked it or not.

My parents got out a globe and showed us where Michigan and Maine were located, and then all the way across the Atlantic Ocean, in between France and Germany, they pointed to a small country named Belgium. They told us that they spoke French and Flemish in Belgium. I had no idea what Flemish was but later learned it was a Dutch dialect as Belgium was just south of the Netherlands.

Katie and I sat and just listened to my parents talk. I don't think we really had any clue as to where we were really going; we just knew it was far away. Katie was only in kindergarten, so I don't think she cared. They told us we were only moving there for three to five years, and we would most likely move back to Michigan. Mom also told us that every summer we would get to come back to the States.

My parents explained that we would go to a school just like we did in Michigan, we would speak English, and there would be other

American and English speaking children in our school. Turns out it wasn't just like our Michigan school.

Our new school was St. John's, a private Catholic school located in Waterloo, which was just outside of Brussels. The principal was Sr. Mary John, and our teachers were also Sisters and Brothers. Although, there were a few who were just Mr. and Mrs. Names, too. We attended a Catholic church, so that was okay, but we had gone to a public school in Midland.

At our new Catholic school, we also had to wear a uniform consisting of bottle green sweaters, grey pleated skirts, a white blouse, green or white socks, and black or brown shoes. I wasn't so impressed. Only about 50 percent of the kids in the school were American. The students came from states and countries all over the world. I had friends from the Carolinas, New Jersey, California, Texas, Connecticut, Wisconsin, Chicago, England, Tehran, Louisiana, Minnesota, Singapore, and Kenya, just to name a few.

My father went to Brussels first in the early spring and was there for the months of March and April. In April, my mom met him in Brussels for a couple of weeks and found a place for us to live. We stayed with family friends and kept going to school. I still didn't realize how far away they actually were, or how far away we were moving.

My mom came back to Midland, the movers came, and the house was packed up. We had to put all of our clothes in piles outside of our dressers, and she made us get rid of some of our stuff.

"If you haven't used it in a year, you don't need it," Mom said. I find myself saying that to my kids now.

The contents of the house fit into the back of a semi truck, or an international shipping container, as the movers explained to us. Our belongings would be going on a boat and, and it would take about eight weeks for everything to arrive in Belgium.

My mom, Katie, Giffie and I left Michigan at the end of April and went to Maine to spend time with our grandparents and other family members before we embarked on this journey. Nana seemed nervous about us moving so far away and to a place where English wasn't spoken. She was also upset we were flying so far and over the huge

Atlantic Ocean. Nana didn't like airplanes and had only visited us once in Michigan.

Everyone kept assuring us that this was going to be a fantastic adventure and we were going to gain so much knowledge from living in a foreign country. My mom's sister and her family had moved to Italy in the 1960s, so I think that helped my parents and the rest of the family believe this was no big deal -- kind of like moving to another state. Many people in Maine who had grown up in that state, moved away for jobs, as the job market in Maine continually declined.

At the end of May, my dad came to Maine so my mom wouldn't have to fly alone across the Atlantic Ocean with three kids. We had a ton of luggage, including two suitcases only packed with provisions, to last us a whole year. In the suitcases we had deodorant, Crest© tooth paste, peanut butter, Pop-Tarts©, Lucky Charms© cereal, and Agree© and Breck© shampoo, since we couldn't buy any of those things in Brussels. We had learned this information from other Americans with my dad's company who were living in Brussels. The schools also helped us know what we might want to bring from the U.S. that would not be available in Europe. There were A LOT of American things I would find out that I couldn't buy in Brussels. Nana also packed us a snack bag for the plane filled with our favorite whoopie pies.

On this trip we weren't dressed in pajamas, because we had to "look nice," according to my mom. I wore a pair of red denim bell bottoms, my favorite red paisley smocked shirt, and my new brown wedges that were for me to wear with my Catholic uniform.

We flew from Bangor, Maine, to New York's John F. Kennedy airport. From New York, we flew to London's Heathrow airport and got off our Pan Am flight. It was a very long eight-hour flight, and I felt like I had the flu. My dad told us we were almost to Brussels, but we had to stay awake for the rest of the day and we would feel fine tomorrow. I think it was more like four days before the 'flying flu' (jet lag) was gone. In London, we left for Brussels on SABENA airlines. Many of us who lived in Brussels over the years said SABENA stood for Such A Bad Experience Never Again. On June 1, 1976, we touched down in the Brussels airport and our European adventure began.

My parents always showed an image of extreme confidence in what they were doing, never acting afraid or timid of a new experience, so we acted the same. We were up for any new experience. I hope I have given that to my children as well.

BLUEBERRY
WHOOPIE PIES

BLUEBERRY
HOT FUDGE SAUCE

Blueberry Whoopie Pies

Serves 10

½ cup butter at room temperature
1 cup, plus 3 tablespoons, light brown sugar
1 tablespoon grated lemon zest
1 teaspoon vanilla
1 egg
2¼ cup flour
¾ teaspoon baking soda
½ teaspoon salt
1 cup whole milk
¾ cup heavy cream
1 cup fresh blueberries

Preheat oven to 350˚

In a large bowl, using an electric mixer, beat butter, 1 cup brown sugar, and lemon zest until light and creamy. Add vanilla, egg and combine. In a medium bowl, whisk together, flour, baking powder, baking soda, and salt. With mixer on low, beat in flour mixture in three additions, alternating with milk and ending with the flour mixture. Mix all ingredients well to combine. Drop batter in 2 tablespoon mounds, about 2 inches apart, onto two parchment-lined baking sheets. Bake until puffed and pale golden around edges, 17-19 minutes. Let cool completely.

In a small bowl, mash blueberries with a fork, or you can use a Blueberry Haven Jam of your choice, instead of the blueberries. Fold into the heavy cream.

Divide the blueberry cream evenly and spread on half of the cakes, then top with the other half of the cakes to form a sandwich.

Blueberry Hot Fudge Sauce

Serves 4

6 tablespoons flour
2 cups sugar
2/3 cups cocoa
2 cups milk
2 tablespoons butter
2 teaspoons vanilla
2 teaspoons blueberry simple syrup (or Blueberry Haven
Blueberry Elixir)

Mix dry ingredients in a saucepan. Add milk and cook over
low heat until thick. Remove from heat and add butter,
vanilla and blueberry simple syrup. Cool and store in
refrigerator. Makes 2 pints.

Traveling & Living in Europe

During our time in Brussels, my parents made the most of our experience and there were many weekends when we were "traveling across Europe on $10 a day," as my parents would say. That was also a book, Europe On $10 A Day, which traveled with us as we went on many of our excursions. And although it doesn't sound possible, we went to London by car.

We would all climb into the Toyota Corolla station wagon my sister and I called 'diarrhea brown,' fighting over who got to sit in the way back, which we thought was the best seat in the car. It didn't even have a seat, just a piece of brown flecked carpeting that we would lie on.

My father would drive our entire family to Calais in France, about an hour and a half drive. There the car would be put on a Hovercraft to cross the English Channel. The first time I saw the Hovercraft coming up on the beach in Calais was very exciting. I didn't know what to expect of a boat we were putting our car on, but the Hovercraft came right up on the beach like it was an amphibian crawling out of the water. The hover part looked like a big car tire inflated and deflated, and the whole boat just hovered over the water as it traveled. My dad drove our car onto the Hovercraft, and we all loaded on the boat.

As to be expected, the English Channel waves were white caps, and the weather was a misty grey, just like it was anytime we ever visited England. It took about two hours and was pretty uneventful until we started to see the shoreline of England, or the White Cliffs of Dover, where the Hovercraft docked, in Dover, England. They were huge sand cliffs that were as white as snow and a majestic sight. The Hovercraft went up on the land, deflated its big inner tube, and off we drove toward London in our station wagon.

While in London, we stayed at a small boutique hotel that was clean and had a comfortable bed. I'm sure it was listed in the Europe On $10 A day book, but my mom always told us we weren't there to hang out in our hotel room, as there was a lot to see and do. So, off we went.

In London we always went to the theatre, and on our first trip (at the age of 12), I saw Annie and Oklahoma. They were both fantastic!

I also learned how to shop in London. My mom, who has a great sense of style and taste, always knew just the places to shop: Mark's and Spencer, and Harrods were the big department stores we hit. We also shopped in many little boutiques along the way. My favorite purchase ever was my beautiful bedroom linens my mom kept on my bed until that bed ended up in my married house. It was a white ruffled duvet set with Swiss pink dots and adorned with pink roses. I loved it.

When in London, we also did what Londoners did and had lunch in the cafeteria at Mark's and Spencer. Dinner was in a typical English pub where we ate lots of fish and chips, and we always smothered our chips in lots of vinegar. We were also introduced to a fantastic British dessert called the Eton Mess. I still make it to this day, and it is everyone's favorite.

We also took a tour in a "double decker buser," which is what Giffie called the bright red double deck busses that are the public transportation all over London. We saw Buckingham Palace and the changing of the guards. I loved the look of the big beefeater hats the guards wore, how stiff they marched, and just "how British they are," as my dad said. We also saw Westminster Abbey and Big Ben. London truly was a magical city, even if the whole time we were visiting we had our umbrellas up.

After a long weekend in London, I couldn't wait to get back to my English speaking school and my many British friends to let them know I had seen the big city of their country. About thirty percent of the students at St. John's were British, as were many of our teachers. I can still sing the British National Anthem, God loves the Queen.

GRAND HAVEN MESS

MERINGUE COOKIES

BLUEBERRY QUINOA SALAD
with LEMON BASIL DRESSING

Grand Haven Mess

Serves 8

20 Meringue cookies, crumbled
3 cups fresh blueberries
2 cups fresh raspberries
1 tablespoon Frangelico
1 container of Cool Whip©

Crumble about 10 meringue cookies and layer in the bottom of a glass bowl. In a sauté pan, combine 1 cup blueberries, 1 cup raspberries and 1 tablespoon Frangelico©. Bring this to a rolling boil. Pour into a bowl and cool in the refrigerator for about a half hour (you can do this ahead). Once cool, pour the mixture over the layer of cookies, add a layer of Cool Whip©, top with fresh blueberries and raspberries, add another layer of meringue cookies crumbled, Cool Whip©, and top with the leftover berries.

As an alternative, you can purchase our Blueberry Haven Blueberry Jam and use this as your layer over the meringue. Heat it first until warm.

- -

Meringue Cookies

Makes about 20 cookies

4 egg whites
Pinch of salt
¼ teaspoon cream of tartar
1 1/3 cup sugar

Preheat oven to 275°

In large bowl, whip the egg whites with salt and cream of tartar; slowly sprinkle in the sugar until they whip into peaks.

Drop large spoonfuls onto cookie sheets covered with parchment paper. Bake for about 35 minutes. Let cool.

Blueberry Quinoa Salad with Lemon Basil Dressing

Serves 4

Quinoa:
½ cup quinoa
1 cup water

Fruits and veggies:
1 cup fresh blueberries
½ cup cubed cucumbers
½ tablespoon Blueberry Haven Dried Blueberries

Lemon basil dressing:
1½ tablespoons extra virgin olive oil
2 tablespoons lemon juice
¼ teaspoon lemon zest
10 basil leaves, finely chopped
Salt and pepper

Place the quinoa and water in a medium skillet and bring to a boil. Reduce heat and simmer covered for about 15 minutes or until the quinoa is cooked. Remove the lid, and fluff the quinoa with a fork. Let it cool to room temperature.

While the quinoa is cooking, combine the fruit in a bowl and refrigerate until you are ready to serve the salad.

Whisk together all the dressing ingredients, except the chopped basil. Refrigerate until you are ready to serve. Chop and add the basil to the dressing just before serving. If you add it earlier, it will turn black. Add half the dressing to the quinoa and mix gently.

Assemble the salad just before serving: toss the quinoa, fruit and cucumbers together. Dish up the other half of the dressing on the side. Serve immediately.

A Real Life Education Abroad

I don't know if it was lucky or unlucky for us, but our parents took us to many of the not-so-great sights of Europe. During the time we lived in Europe, there was East Germany and West Germany. Being young and having heard of World War II and what the Holocaust meant, I was not excited to see the sights where so much grief was inflicted on the human race.

We took a field trip at St. John's to the concentration camp named Buchenwald, located in Belgium, and I had a sick feeling in my stomach during the whole tour. Our tour guide had been a prisoner at the camp during the war and shared with us many vivid and gruesome ways in which people were tortured at the camp. The examples of torture he explained to us during our tour were so horrific, I will never forget them.

One long weekend, my parents decided we should visit the city of West Berlin. To get there from Belgium, we had to drive across West Germany and into East Germany until we got to West Berlin. I was 13, Katie was nine and Giffie was five. We didn't think the trip would be a big deal as we had been traveling around Europe for three years. We had no idea what we were about to encounter. Traveling through West Germany was just like normal, and when we got to the border of Belgium, my dad flashed our five American passports to the border guard and we continued on our way. By this time, my dad had upgraded vehicles and we now had a white diesel Mercedes. Katie and I were so glad to be rid of the embarrassing diarrhea brown Toyota. All three of us kids were sitting next to each another in the back seat -- me behind my dad, Giffie in the middle and Katie behind my mom.

As the car slowed about a half mile from the border into East Germany, my dad said in his most stern voice, "You three had better not make one sound, and you better not even blink as this is VERY SERIOUS as we go through the border."

Katie and I looked at each other.

"Okay, dad," I said.

We knew that if his voice was that stern we better sit like statues. As we got closer to the border and the guard booth, we could see what looked like large road signs along both sides of the entrance. They were actually large mirrors so the guards could see each person's every move. We pulled up to the gate and my dad handed the guard our passports. The guard was wearing tall, black, shiny boots, a military uniform, and was carrying a HUGE machine gun. My mom mumbled, "Kids, do not move," very quietly so the guard couldn't hear her. As the guard at the booth was asking my dad the nature of our traveling though East Germany, there were four other guards on all corners of our car. Each of them had a device on wheels they were sticking up under our car and I wondered what they were doing. They opened all our car doors to confirm there were only five of us in the car, and then they opened the hood and the trunk of the car. Giffie, Katie and I were scared to death and sat perfectly still. I kept thinking of the stories the tour guide at Buchenwald had told us, and this guard looked like what I thought a Nazi would look like. As the guards were going around our car, they talked in sharp, clipped tones. I wished I spoke German so I knew what they were saying. After what seemed like 30 minutes of sitting like perfect mannequins, the guard returned all five passports to my dad and let us go into East Germany.

Once we were about 20 miles down the road, my parents began to talk again. They too had been quite scared, and I'm sure they were wondering what they were doing taking themselves and their three kids into a communist country. They explained to us that the device on wheels was a mirror, and it was used to see if people were curled in the wheel wells of our car trying to sneak into East Germany, as many German families had been separated by the dividing of Germany after World War II.

The drive along the autobahn in East Germany was not eventful, but we never saw any other cars or people, and that was a little creepy. In West Germany, there were great German cars whizzing by at unprecedented speeds as we passed the many ausfahrts along the autobahn. As kids, we always got a huge kick out of the word ausfahrt, which means exit in German.

Once we arrived in West Berlin, we had to go through the border control, mirrors, and guards with German Shepherd dogs all over again, but this time we weren't as scared because we knew what to expect. West Berlin was just like the rest of what we knew of

West Germany, and we stayed at the bed and breakfast of a very nice German couple. There were crisp linens on the bed I slept on, which was just a mattress in what I called a closet. Of course my mom reminded me again that we weren't here to stay in our hotel. Since we were staying in someone's house, my mom wanted us to be extra grateful to the family who welcomed us into their home. For breakfast, our fräulein had prepared yogurts, cheese, boiled eggs, hard rolls and jams for us. There was also a sweet that reminded me of some sort of strudel.

During our visit in West Berlin, we took a tour bus into East Berlin where we had to cross through the border of the city at the Great Berlin Wall. The East Germans came onto the tour bus with their mirrored devices and checked every seat and every passenger. Again, it was very intimidating.

Once in East Berlin, we saw the people of East Germany and how they lived. I will never forget asking my dad, "Why are all the cars exactly the same, except for a different color? Why are all the houses exactly the same and how come none of the people are smiling or even look happy?"

"This is a communist country and it is how they live," my dad said. "The people are all treated the same."

I don't think I understood what he had said to me back then when I was only 13 years old. It wasn't until I was watching the tearing down of the Berlin Wall as an adult that I truly understood. I felt so sorry for the people who lived on the other side of the wall who didn't look very happy, and to me, I knew it would be strange to live in a country where everything was the same.

I lived in Brussels from 1976-1981, during the ages of ten to fifteen, which was a huge part of my maturing process. I believe that during those years, you become a lot of the person you are as an adult, and before that you don't really have an opinion on life, people, or the circumstances around your life. Around fifth grade, you start paying attention to yourself and compare yourself to others in your life. I feel so lucky to have been exposed to so many different people at a young age. From my experiences, I know people of all different faiths, ethnicities, and sexual orientations. They are no different than myself and most others I've met through my many travels.

I can't imagine the person I would be today without the many people I encountered throughout our time in Brussels.

Going to school with kids from so many different places really made me think differently than if I had grown up in one town, one school, and one church. I have many different groups of friends to thank for opening my eyes to the different cultures that exist in the United States and throughout the world. I had my southern contingent of friends who were from Louisiana, North Carolina, South Carolina and Texas. From them I learned a slower style of life and talk, impeccable manners, an appreciation for southern cooking, big southern families, and southern nicknames. One of my friend's mom's name was Cookie. I just love that her name was Cookie and to this day I don't know her real name. And how does a boy named Walter have a nickname like Jeb? My two best friends, when they left Brussels, moved back to the metro New York area, and from their families I learned about big city living, a New York lifestyle, exquisite clothing, live-in help, private boarding schools and what a corporate 'bigwig' meant. From the Minnesota contingent, many of whom lived in our neighborhood in Belgium, there were typical Minnesota families with typical

Scandinavian last names like Thompson and Richelson. Many of the Minnesota boys had a rough time when moving to Brussels where there was no hockey. They said their lives revolved around 3M (Minnesota, Mining and Manufacturing Company) where their dads were employed, White Bear Lake and hockey.

I had real Scandinavian friends (who hailed from Denmark, Sweden), who were beautiful with blonde hair, blue eyes and porcelain skin, yet they had no clue of their beauty. The British kids had their funny accents and pointed out that each of their accents were different because they came from different areas in England. I could never tell the difference as they all sounded British to me. I loved my British girlfriends, their horses and British style of riding, how prim they were, and how they took their tea and crumpets. There were kids from the continent of Africa -- Kenya and Tanzania -- and many who had moved and lived in the Middle East, Tehran and Saudi Arabia. They shared their stories of being foreigners living in Saudi Arabia.

With NATO headquartered in Brussels, there were diplomat children from all over the world. Yet at the age of 10, I didn't really understand what it meant when someone said, "Natalie's dad is the Ambassador to Ireland," or "So and so's dad is the president of this major corporation." We were all just friends and expats living in a foreign country, going to school together and playing on sports teams together. It didn't matter where you were from or who you were; we were a big St. John's Family -- Christian, Catholic or otherwise. I didn't realize how special all of this was until I was back in a public school in the middle of the Mitten State in the Midwest.

BLUEBERRY
YOGURT PARFAIT

BLUEBERRY
STRUDEL

Blueberry Yogurt Parfait

Serves 1

½ cup plain Greek yogurt, fat-free
1 tablespoon white balsamic vinegar
1 tablespoon Blueberry Haven Blossom Honey
1 cup of blueberries

Combine yogurt, vinegar and honey in a small bowl and mix together well. In a small jelly jar, layer the yogurt sauce first, then the blueberries, and continue until jar is full, finishing with the blueberries on top. Refrigerate 2-3 hours before serving.

Blueberry Strudel

Serves 4

1 sheet of puff pastry
¼ cup small curd cottage cheese
¼ cup plain Greek yogurt
4 oz cream cheese
2½ tablespoons of Blueberry Haven Jam, any flavor (we used Blueberry Haven Blueberry Jam)
Fresh blueberries
Powdered sugar

Preheat oven to 350°

Mix cottage cheese, yogurt and cream cheese together in a bowl; fold in blueberries. Place puff pastry on a cookie sheet and spread mixture on top. Roll the pastry. Bake at 350° for 40 minutes. Slice; sprinkle with powdered sugar, fresh blueberries and serve.

The Luddens - Family Friends

During the school year from September to June, my family lived in Belgium, but every summer we ventured back to the States. My mom always joked that we were like a band of gypsies. We would pack light on our way back home to the U.S., knowing we would be coming back to Brussels with our suitcases bulging with our most favorite American items. We thought we 'needed' things like toothpaste, shampoo and deodorant to survive for the next school year. There would be a stack of plane tickets an inch deep for each of us as we went on our way to the U.S. for the entire summer.

The summer often consisted of us traversing the United States; however, the majority of our time was spent at the Neeland Camp on Cold Stream Pond. As my siblings, cousins and I got older; we were given a bigger roaming area on the lake. Most of the time we stayed between the Ludden Camp and the Neeland Camp, although I spent weeks at a time at the Ludden Camp with my cousin Jill. The Ludden Camp was my cousin Jill's grandparents' camp. Jill's mom was my Aunt Valerie, my mother's oldest sister. Jill's grandmother, (I called her Mrs. Ludden), always welcomed me with Jill down to their camp.

During the school year, Jill lived in Falmouth, Maine, which was a small town and suburb of Portland, Maine. Jill and I were only 18 months apart in age, and growing up we spent a lot of time together. Mrs. Ludden, before retiring, had been an English teacher. She gave me my great love of reading as there was not much television down to camp. She would often ask me my reading interest, and sure enough, out would come a book. I enjoyed every book she chose for me to read. I think she started me off with the Nancy Drew books, and I devoured them. Then I went on to read the Hardy Boys books. There were many times in the summer when you could find me with a book on the dock, on the porch in a rocking chair, or just lying on my bed reading.

Today I am guilty of shutting people out when I am reading a good book. I don't think Mrs. Ludden would think that was so bad. To me she was an exceptional lady as she challenged me and Jill to watch out for ourselves and for others, and to be smart. She always asked us lots of questions about situations that could happen in life. She also gave us advice on how we could help others less fortunate than ourselves.

All summer long there were people coming and going at the Ludden camp and most were extended family members. Many people came down to camp to see John, Mrs. Ludden's youngest son and Jill's uncle. John was born with Downs Syndrome, and during the school year he lived away at a special school. I don't remember camp without John, and he would give me and Jill many good laughs! I can thank him for my reading, also, as down to camp the television only received three stations. Of those three stations, John would only let the TV be on Channel 5, which carried all of John's favorite shows. Everyone knew not to even try to change the station and sneak one by John, as he knew the programs of every channel down to every minute. So, Jill and I resorted to reading books.

John also had a stack of photographs that were always next to him on the red wooden camp couch. He looked through these photos while watching Channel 5. Over the years, the photos had become blurry and you couldn't tell who was in the picture, but John knew. He would go though his pictures one by one and tell us who was in each picture and what they were doing. The pictures were of family and friends that had been taken throughout the previous 10 to 15 years and John always had them in order. I believe the photos made John feel as if his family was always with him. Once, Jill and I got the pictures and put them in a different order, but John could still tell us who was in each picture.

Jill, John and I used to jump off the dock into the lake at Cold Stream. We would try to get John to go in first to tell us if the water was cold, and sometimes he would trick us and tell us the water wasn't cold. Then we would jump in and yell, "John, it's freezing." He would laugh at us and be so happy that he had tricked us into running off the dock to jump in rather than wading in inch by inch.

John's favorite treat was Mrs. Ludden's fantastic peanut butter fudge because it was creamy and delicious. Her fudge was a favorite of mine and I couldn't wait to have it when I was at the Ludden camp. I smile when I think of John, and today at 60 he is still alive. I'm not sure how much he goes down to camp anymore, but knowing Jill's Uncle Doug, who now is the owner of the Ludden Camp and still spends time at Cold Stream, I bet John gets there once in awhile.

TURKEY SLIDERS
with BLUEBERRY KETCHUP

COLD STREAM
PEANUT BUTTER and
BLUEBERRY JAM FUDGE

Turkey Sliders with Blueberry Ketchup

Serves 4-6

2 lbs ground turkey
3 tablespoons olive oil
1 tablespoon Blueberry Haven Blueberry Honey Mustard
1 teaspoon thyme leaves
Salt and pepper to taste
Mini buns, tomato, and lettuce

Combine turkey, olive oil, honey mustard and thyme leaves
in a bowl and mix together. Season with salt and pepper.
Form into patties and grill. Serve with Blueberry Ketchup.

Blueberry Ketchup

Serves 4-6

2½ cups blueberries
1 cup brown sugar
½ cup chopped sweet onion
1/3 cup white balsamic vinegar
1 tablespoon minced ginger
¼ teaspoon salt

In a medium sauce pan over medium heat, combine
blueberries, brown sugar, onion, vinegar, ginger and salt;
heat until all sugar has dissolved. Lower the heat so the
mixture is simmering and cook, stirring until blueberries
pop and the ketchup is thickening. Remove from heat and
set aside; it will thicken as it cools.

Cold Stream Peanut Butter and Blueberry Jam Fudge

Serves 8

2 cups granulated sugar
¾ cup evaporated milk
1½ cup peanut butter
2 cups marshmallow fluff
1 teaspoon vanilla extract
2 tablespoons butter
½ cup Blueberry Haven Jam

In a medium saucepan, add the sugar and evaporated milk, stirring constantly until the mixture reaches a full boil. Continue at a rolling boil for 5 minutes. Remove from the cook top and quickly add the peanut butter, vanilla, and marshmallow fluff until all is mixed together. Swirl in each corner a teaspoon of Blueberry Haven Jam.

Down East in Machias, Maine

Machias, Maine, is a very small town on the east coast of Maine. My cousins lived there, and during our yearly summer visits to Maine, we loved to take a trip over to see them. First on our agenda when we got to Machias was to go down to the docks to get lobster for "suppah." Their house was located just a few miles from the ocean, where many of the lobster fishermen would dock their lobster boats. We would go down to the docks and see the boats and all the lobsters the fishermen had caught. Lobster boats looked like mini tug boats with flat bottoms and long back ends. Often they were painted in bright colors of blue, green and red. We would walk right out onto the wooden docks next to the lobster boats, and in the salt water next to their boats were huge chests we thought were treasure chests. They were often filled to the brim with lobsters. The fishermen would pull the lobster traps out of the water, lift off the cover and let us choose any lobsters we wanted to take home. There are no fresher tasting lobsters than ones that have just come out of a lobsterman's trap.

If the tide was still out on our way back to our cousin's house, we would rake for a few clams to take back for dinner. Taking our clam rakes, we would walk down to where the ocean sand and water broke and where the sand was still quite wet. A clam rake looks similar to a down east wild blueberry rake. The rake part has metal prongs that make a flat bottom. You hold onto the rake by a handle that comes out over the metal prongs, making it more like a scooping rake. At the ocean, we would stick our rake in and scoop up a bunch of sand. If we were lucky, we would have a few clams in our rake each time we scooped. We would pick the clams out of our rake, toss them in a bucket and keep scooping until our bucket was full. This was always great fun and an excuse to get muddy.

Once we had our lobsters picked and our clam buckets full, we would head back so the lobsters and clams could be cooked for dinner. While the grown-ups were getting the flames ready for the 'lobstah' and 'steamahs,' the kids would take the rakes and go out to the fields of wild blueberry bushes that were in the back of the house. There we would scoop and scoop until our buckets were full of blueberries. Of course, we would eat some while we were picking and throw a few at each other, as well. Wild Maine blueberries are small in size, but big and tart in flavor. Once our some while we were picking and throw a few at each other, as well. Wild Maine blueberries are small in size, but big and tart in flavor. Once our buckets were full, we would walk back up to the house and hand over the blueberries so that a scrumptious blueberry dessert could be made. Often it was a big bowl of blueberry trifle.

Usually just as we would be getting back from picking the berries, the lobsters were being pulled out of the big pots. Lobsters were cooked in big boiling pots over an open flame, and once the water was boiling, the lobsters were dropped in until they were a bright red. And, no, I've never heard a lobster scream.

After the steamers (clams) were scrubbed clean of all the ocean sand and salt, they were put in another pot of boiling water, usually with garlic, chives and green onions.

If the weather permitted, we would eat around picnic tables adorned with red-and-white-check tablecloths, napkins and the traditional lobster plastic bib. Every place setting would have silverware, nut crackers, lobster crackers, a small metal pick and fork to pick the lobster meat out of all the small crevices, and a dipping bowl of freshly melted butter. On our plates would be a fully cooked bright red lobster and a bowl of clams. Large, tin bowls sat in the middle of every table for the shells.

In Maine, from the time you could sit at a table you learned to clean and eat your own lobster, as well as pick the clams right out of the shells.

STEAMED
LOBSTERS

STEAMED CLAMS

BLUEBERRY HAVEN
TRIFLE

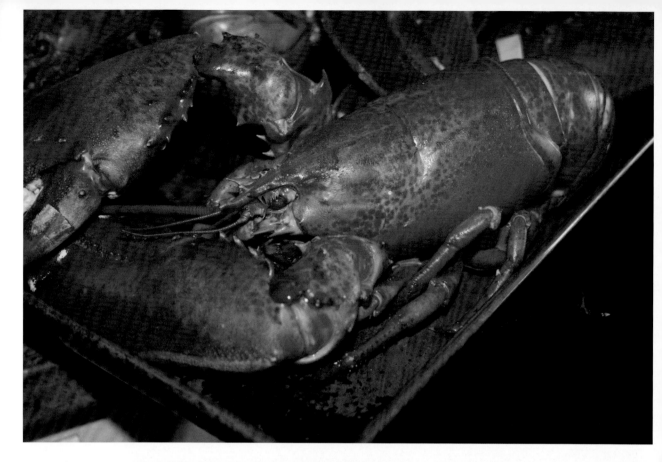

Steamed Lobster

Lobster(s)
Pinch of salt
Lemon juice
Butter (melted)

Fill a large pot (we love using our Michigan Turkey Fryer --
works great) half way with water; add salt to the water and
bring to a boil. Once the water is boiling, put in the lobsters
and cover tightly with a lid. Let the water return to a boil.
Generally lobsters take about 13 minutes per pound for the
first pound; add 3 minutes per pound for each additional
pound. A 1.5 pound lobster will cook for about 14 minutes.

Serve with melted butter, or just a bit of squeezed lemon
juice.

Steamed Clams

Serves 6

1 tablespoon Light Olive Oil
½ cup parsley, chopped
¼ cup celery, chopped
2 tablespoons garlic, chopped
¼ cup white wine -- I use chardonnay
1 cup broth -- I use a cup from the steamed lobster pot
Dash of pepper
4 lbs of clams

In a large stock pot, heat olive oil and sauté the garlic for about a minute. Add in the parsley, basil, wine, broth and bring to a boil. Add clams and cover with a lid. Cook about 5 minutes. Stir at least once and cook until all the shells are open. Season with salt and pepper.

Blueberry Haven Trifle

Serves 8

8 oz. cream cheese
½ cup confectioners sugar
14 oz sweetened condensed milk
1 teaspoon vanilla
3.4 oz package instant vanilla pudding
2 cups Cool Whip©
Angel food cake or Blueberry Haven Muffin Mix, cut into
1-inch pieces
2 cups Blueberry Haven fresh blueberries, when in season;
when not in season, use Blueberry Haven Blueberry
Topping.

Mix together cream cheese, sugar, condensed milk, vanilla
and instant pudding mixture. Fold in the Cool Whip©.
In a serving bowl, layer the bread mixture (angel food cake
or blueberry muffins), top with the pudding mixture, then
sprinkle on blueberries or topping. Repeat.

The Armpit of the Thumb & Pointer Finger

In 1981, my family moved to Midland, Michigan. If you were from Michigan, you put your hand up like a mitten and pointed to where your city was located in the Mitten State. Midland was at the armpit of the thumb and the pointer finger, about 40 minutes from Flint and 30 minutes from Saginaw.

After living in Europe for five years, traveling and experiencing all that Europe had to offer, I was NOT excited to live in a town with less than 50,000 people -- no lake, mountain, big-city shopping, culture, or ethnic people.

Midland was pretty much a two-company town and most men worked for either Dow Chemical or Dow Corning. Dow Chemical families were the big brother to Dow Corning, so my dad's job was at the little sister company. Moving to a new school, even though I had lived in Midland before, was very difficult. Being the new girl in 10th grade was not easy as life was very different living in Midland versus living in Brussels, Belgium.

My saving grace while I was at Dow High was yearbook. I was on the yearbook staff all three years, and during my senior year, Mrs. Rosten, the advisor, chose me to be the editor. Like me, at one point in her life, she had lived overseas and I think she understood what I was going through.

During my sophomore year, I really struggled and didn't have many friends, except my teammates on cross country, gymnastics, and track. Even those friends had friends they had known all their lives, so I was always just a third wheel. It seemed like everybody had a boyfriend, too.

My junior year I had a boyfriend, and I think that helped me fit in a little better. I had friends who dated my boyfriend's friends, so I was included in some of the 'cooler' events. My boyfriend was a very nice guy, from a nice family, and he played football, hockey and baseball. Watching all his sports was a diversion in my high school experience. The hockey team had a great year that year and went all the way to the state quarter finals. I find it ironic that a kid on that team would one day, as an adult, became one of my son's hockey coaches. I had a few girlfriends and we would go to all the boys' games to cheer them on. I was thankful the Minnesota boys had given me a clue about hockey and what the blue line meant. It is the offsides line and the puck must go over the blue line before the players, or you, are considered off sides.

We went on many great road trips all over the state. Hockey road trips to the Grand Rapids area to play East Kentwood High School was my first introduction to the west side of Michigan.

Thankfully, I had Mrs. Rosten and yearbook during my junior year. I admired her as she dressed more stylish than the other teachers. I thought she held her head higher, but I now understand she was just more worldly. Like me, she too had lived in Europe with her family at a younger age.

The summer before my senior year I visited colleges in the state of Michigan. It seemed that people from the town of Midland rarely left the state to go to college. Most everyone I knew went to Michigan State, Central Michigan, and Western Michigan. A few went to smaller schools as well -- mostly Albion. Dow had a big presence there and Dow Corning had a big presence at Hope College. I had gone to yearbook camp at Michigan State and felt that a big school was not the place for me.

I think my Mom at that time was afraid I wasn't going to go anywhere, so she suggested looking at some smaller schools. I visited Albion, Aquinas and Hope. I liked both Albion and Hope and thought Hope had a pretty campus, pretty people, and Lake Michigan nearby. I spent a weekend at Albion in the early fall with my girlfriend, Jennifer, on campus and had a blast. She had been a year ahead of me at Dow High and was a freshman at Albion. Since it was only September and I still had to finish my senior year, I had plenty of time to decide on a college.

At the beginning of October of my senior year, my dad came home from work and we sat down for a dinner of my mom's delicious crispy baked chicken, a salad (always a given every night) and some sort of potato. My grandfather was Joseph Patrick O'Leary, so potatoes were a staple in our house.

"Kids, I've taken a new job in the Orient," my dad said.

Giffie, who was now 10 years old and in the fourth grade, made his eyes slanted and said, "We are Siamese, if you please."

We had two Siamese cats at the time. I don't think my dad thought that was very funny, as he rolled his eyes at Giffie and lifted his eyebrows at my mom. He went on to explain that his job would be in Tokyo and there was an American school in Japan that Katie and Giffie would be attending. I was looking at him dumbfounded and wondering what I would be doing in Midland with no one but 'framily' (thank goodness for framily) to care about me. Framily was a combination of friends that acted more like family. Framily was also, many times, more fun to hang out with because all the 'family' stuff didn't come with them. Here we go again, I thought; however, I was secretly excited that my brother and sister were going to get out of Michigan and go to a cool, HUGE city.

I just wasn't sure where I was going to end up.

CRISPY BLUEBERRY
HAVEN MUSTARD
CHICKEN

MICHIGAN BLUE
CHEESE BLUEBERRY
SALAD

BLUEBERRY
VINAIGRETTE

BLUEBERRY
BISCUITS

Crispy Blueberry Haven
Mustard Chicken

Serves 4-5

4-6 garlic cloves
2 tablespoons minced marjoram leaves
Sea salt and freshly ground pepper
2 cups panko bread crumbs
1 tablespoon lemon zest
2 tablespoons olive oil
2 tablespoons unsalted butter, melted
½ cup Blueberry Haven Honey Mustard
½ cup dry white wine -- I use chardonnay
4-6 medium-sized chicken breasts

Preheat oven to 350°

In food processor, mince the garlic, marjoram salt and
pepper until finely minced. Add the bread crumbs, lemon
zest, olive oil and butter and process until combined. Put all
of this in a bowl. In another bowl whisk together the wine
and Blueberry Haven Honey Mustard.

Rinse and pat dry the chicken. Dip the chicken first in the
wine/mustard mixture and then coat in the crumb mixture.
Place the chicken on a greased sheet pan. Bake for 40
minutes at 350°. Raise the heat to 400° and bake another 10
minutes, until crumbs are browned.

Michigan Blue Cheese Blueberry Salad with Blueberry Vinaigrette

Serves 4-6

1 head romaine lettuce, torn into bite-sized pieces
¾ cup crumbled Blue Cheese
¼ cup chopped red onion
Cracked black pepper to taste
½ cup Blueberry Haven Dried Blueberries

In a large bowl, place torn romaine, blue cheese, red onion and cracked pepper. Sprinkle with dried blueberries and 1 cup candied pecans.

Candied pecans
1 egg white
1 tablespoon water
1 pound pecan halves
1 cup granulated sugar
¾ teaspoon salt
½ teaspoon ground cinnamon

Preheat oven to 250°

For candied pecans: beat egg white and water until frothy. In a separate bowl, combine sugar, salt and cinnamon. Add pecans to egg whites, stirring to coat nuts evenly. Remove nuts and toss in sugar mixture until coated. Spread on greased baking sheet. Bake at 250° for about 1 hour, stirring every 15 minutes. Cool.

Blueberry Vinaigrette
(or use Blueberry Haven Blueberry Balsamic
Garlic Vinaigrette)

Serves 4-6

½ cup olive oil
¼ cup red wine vinegar
2 tablespoons balsamic vinegar
1 clove garlic, minced
2 teaspoons Dijon mustard
½ teaspoon salt, or to taste
¼ teaspoon black pepper
½ cup blueberries, fresh or frozen, then thawed

Combine olive oil, red wine vinegar, balsamic vinegar, garlic,
mustard, salt and pepper in jar with screw-top lid. Shake
until blended. Add blueberries. Chill until served. Dressing
makes 1 ½ cups.

Blueberry Biscuits

Makes about 12 biscuits

2 cups all-purpose flour
2 teaspoons baking powder
2 teaspoons sugar
4 tablespoons butter or margarine
¾ cup buttermilk
1 egg
1 cup fresh blueberries (can use dried or frozen)

Preheat oven to 425°

In a bowl, mix flour, baking powder and sugar together with a whisk. Cut butter into mixture. In a separate bowl, beat egg and milk; add to the dry ingredients and mix together. Fold in blueberries.

Flour a surface and pat dough to about ½ inch thickness. Cut out dough with biscuit cutter. Place biscuit dough on a baking sheet that has been sprayed with cooking spray. Bake 15-20 minutes, until biscuits are golden brown. This makes about 12 biscuits.

We love these with butter and Blueberry Haven Blossom Honey!

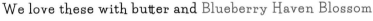

We Are Moving to Japan - Except Me

When my dad made the announcement about my family moving to Tokyo, I needed to decide what I was going to do. At the time he took the job, I had already started getting my college acceptance letters in the mail. I had been accepted to Hope College, and that was my first choice.

My parents had several ideas about what I could do when they moved to Tokyo. There were universities in Tokyo, and colleges on the West Coast or Hawaii that I should consider. Maybe I would want to go to the University of Hawaii, or look at Washington State because my Aunt Mary Ellen and family lived there. Plus, I also would be closer to Japan. They were also willing to get me an apartment in Midland if I wanted to stay there and attend the local community college. I was definitely not staying in Midland as I felt I was ready to move on and start the next stage of my life. I did consider the University of Hawaii, but I knew once I got there I would probably ditch school for the beach. So, I came to the conclusion that I would stick with plan A and attend Hope College in Holland, Michigan.

Throughout our years of living in Midland and overseas, there was another family who experienced the living overseas with us, as well as moving in and out of Midland with us. They were the Hazletons. There were many times through the years, in specific situations, where the Hazletons acted as my parents, and I knew in this situation they would be there for me as well. I would often spend Thanksgiving and Easter break with them and their extended family. There was also a time when Mr. and Mrs. Hazleton were transferred back to Belgium, and their youngest son was a junior in high school and didn't want to move, so he lived with my parents that year. They were fantastic family friends, or as we like to refer to them, framily. The Hazletons were more like my aunt and uncle, and their kids were more like cousins. We spent many holidays together with the Hazleton's throughout our years of living in Brussels and Midland, as we had no extended family in the Midwest. We even called Mrs. Hazleton's mom Maw Maw, just like her grandkids. So, when I went to Hope College, I knew the Hazletons were family I could count on and they would welcome me into their home.

Senior year was no different than any other time in high school: I still had the same boyfriend, and I was the yearbook editor, so I was busy with everything that entailed.

Being yearbook editor helped me decide that I wanted to go into some type of communications, and I was thinking about public relations, advertising or journalism. The college scheduled an interview for me with a professor in the communications department, and after meeting with Dr. Joe McDoniels at Hope College, I chose Hope as my college to attend. My husband loves to tell everyone I went to Hope College with my high school boyfriend, which is partly true. But I think I felt safe because my high school boyfriend's older sister had also gone to Hope, and with my parents being so far away, a small, close-knit group like Hope College offered felt like the perfect choice for me.

As my family prepared for another overseas adventure, I prepared to go to college on the other side of the mitten -- alone.

Our house in Midland was sold, and once again, all our belongings were put in overseas containers and shipped to the Orient. My Mom, Dad, Katie, Giffle, and our two Siamese cats went to Hope College to move me into my freshman dorm room. After they helped me get settled, they would be off for a Japanese immersion for a few weeks in Hawaii and then on to Tokyo. As my parents and I moved all my belongings into my dorm room, Giffie sat on the grass in front of the dorm with our two cat cages. I'm sure my roommate was wondering what she was getting into having me for a roommate.   My dorm room was on the first floor, so Giffie was sitting outside right under my window. At one point I heard him talking, so I looked out and saw him talking to a couple of guys who were obviously upperclassmen. One was wearing an OKE fraternity t-shirt and the other wore a Hope Football t-shirt.

"Hey, what do you have in the cages?" one of the guys asked.

I was thinking this was going to be a great way to meet a football player and fraternity boy, so maybe I should wander outside.

"SNAKES!" Giffie said.

I ducked as quickly as I could to make sure no one knew I was affiliated with the kid with the cages.

Great, I thought, he just blew that chance for me.

This was no different than other times when he would do stuff when there was a boy around me. Once I was being walked to front door of our house after a date and Giffie was peeking out the transom windows on the side, flipping the porch lights on and off. As if boys didn't know I had a little brother!

Once the official start of freshman orientation began, I was on my own and my family was on their way to Tokyo, Japan. Mom, Dad, Katie and Giffie lived there all four years I attended Hope College. My family would, however, spend summers in Glen Arbor (Northern Michigan) where my parents had a summer place. I would live there with them most summers during college.

TIFFANY'S
BLUEBERRY HAVEN
ORIENTAL SPICED
NUTS

CHICKEN SATAY with
BLUEBERRY SAUCE

BLUEBERRY
BOURBON
APPETIZER

HAVEN CREAM PUFFS

Tiffany's Blueberry Haven Oriental Spiced Nuts

Serves 6

8 oz raw cashews

8 oz raw almonds

8 oz raw pecans

8 oz raw peanuts

8 oz. Blueberry Haven Dried Blueberries

4 tablespoons unsalted butter

1½ tablespoons Blueberry Haven Blossom Honey

½ teaspoon chili powder

¼ teaspoon smoked paprika

½ teaspoon freshly ground black pepper

¼ teaspoon cumin

¼ teaspoon cayenne pepper

1 teaspoon Thai fish sauce

Preheat oven to 325°

Make four separate baking trays with one type of nut on each tray. Toast each tray for about 5-10 minutes, until lightly golden brown.

While each tray of nuts are toasting, combine butter and honey in a saucepan. Heat until butter is melted. Transfer to a large bowl and whisk in remaining ingredients. Add all of the toasted nuts and blueberries to the bowl. Toss all together until evenly coated.

Line large baking tray with parchment paper and spread nuts out on tray. Put tray in oven and toast for an additional 5-10 minutes. Check OFTEN to ensure that nuts are not burning. Cool and store in an airtight container if not serving immediately.

Chicken Satay with Blueberry Sauce

Serves 4-6

2 packages of sliced chicken, grilled

Marinade:
2 tablespoons soy sauce
½ teaspoon minced garlic
1 tablespoon chopped fresh cilantro
Vegetable oil

In a bowl, combine soy sauce, garlic, cilantro and vegetable oil; mix well. Slice chicken tenders into thin strips. Place chicken in marinade, coating all sides well. Cover and chill for several hours. After marinating, thread chicken strips on bamboo skewers that have been soaked in water 1 hour. Place skewers on oil grill grate; grill over high heat. Discard marinade. Grill skewers about 10-15 minutes or until chicken is done. Remove from grill and serve with peanut dipping sauce.

Dipping Sauce:
2 tablespoons olive oil
1 tablespoon minced fresh ginger
¼ cup finely chopped onion
2 cloves garlic, crushed
4 tablespoons crunchy peanut butter
½ teaspoon red curry paste
1 tablespoon soy sauce
1/3 cup Blueberry Haven Blueberry Jam
1/3 cup water
Chopped fresh cilantro

In a saucepan, combine olive oil, ginger, onion and garlic. Cook over medium heat until softened. Stir in peanut butter, curry paste, soy sauce, jam and water; mix well. Heat through until mixture is right dipping consistency; add more water, if necessary.

Sprinkle skewers with fresh cilantro and serve with warm peanut/blueberry sauce for dipping.

Blueberry Bourbon Appetizer

Serves 4

1 pound bacon
1 loaf whole wheat bread
1 jar Blueberry Haven Blueberry Chutney
2 tablespoons bourbon
2 tablespoons chives chopped

Cook bacon until crisp and chop into fine pieces. Using a cookie cutter or top of jar, stamp out 1½ inch bread rounds from bread slices. Mix chutney and bourbon; spread chutney mixture on bread rounds, then dip into bacon pieces so they stick to the bread; repeat for all the bread rounds.

Place on a baking sheet and heat under the broiler to make bacon even crispier. Sprinkle with chopped chives and serve.

Haven Cream Puffs

Serves 4-6

1 cup water
½ cup butter
¼ teaspoon salt
4 eggs
2 tablespoons milk
1 egg yolk, lightly beaten
2 cups heavy whipping cream
¼ cup confectioners' sugar
½ teaspoon vanilla extract
1 cup blueberries
Powdered sugar

Preheat oven to 400°

In a saucepan over medium heat, bring water, butter and salt to a boil. Add flour and stir until a ball forms. Remove from heat and let stand for 5 minutes. Add eggs one at time, beating after each addition. Continue beating until mix is smooth and shiny.

Drop ¼ cupfuls of batter a couple inches apart onto greased baking sheets. Mix milk and egg yolk together and brush on puffs. Bake at 400° for 30 -35 minutes until golden brown. Let cool.

In a separate bowl, beat cream until it thickens. Add sugar and vanilla until almost stiff. Fold in blueberries. Split apart cream puffs and discard soft dough that is inside. Fill with the cream just before serving. Dust with powdered sugar. You can substitute the cream filling for an ice cream of your choice and top with the blueberry hot fudge, making them Pam's Porfiterrols. This is a dessert my mom served many times while entertaining.

Staying Connected to Michigan

While my family lived in Tokyo and I was at Hope College, and since we had no computers (just phones and letter writing), I talked to my family every Sunday night. Over my four years at college, many of my friends would love to place the phone call for me just to hear Ijima-san answer the phone. Ijama-san always answered the phone, "Brown Residence -- Ijma-san speaking," in her Japanese accent. My friends thought Ijma-san was our maid as she came during the week to help my mom and family throughout their time in Tokyo. She did help my mom inside the house; however, she did so much more for my family, including staying with my brother and sister if my parents had to go away, picking up dry cleaning, or grocery shopping. My parents knew that with having Ijima-san's help, they had someone who could speak the local language and navigate the city and customs of the Japanese. On my first trip to Tokyo, I was excited to meet her, because my family talked so much about Ijma-san and how helpful she was.

When I saw my dad in early October, it was the first time I had seen a family member since I went to Hope. My dad had meetings in Midland, and I spent time with him at his hotel. It was during this visit in the states that he decided to buy a summer place in Northern Michigan. He had heard of this great place in Northern Michigan called The Homestead, a resort he had heard of during some off-site meetings. At that time, The Homestead was mostly private homes, private condominiums and an inn with a few hotel rooms available. He called my mom and told her he bought a place "Up North." This caught my mom by surprise, because he never did anything without running it by her first. He told her that Northern Michigan was a lot like Maine; we needed an address in the states, and I needed an address for myself for when they were not around. Mom was a little worried that my dad had picked something out without her, and since I was the first person to see the place after my dad bought it, I called her. I gave her a detailed description of what the inside looked like.

"Mom it's great," I said. "It's not decorated how you'd like, but you'll have no problem making it looking like home."

I told her she would love it and she did. The condo turned out to be our favorite place for the next 17 years.

During the four years I was at Hope and my family lived in Tokyo, I used the condo for winter breaks. During the summer months, my family would come home and we would live at the condo together. It wasn't much different than when we lived in Belgium and spent our summers on Cold Stream. To this day, Mom and Dad still have a home in Northern Michigan where they spend summers.

I would fly back and forth to Tokyo mostly on my own to visit my family. I usually went at Christmas during college, and a couple of times I went for spring break and a few weeks of summer break. Traveling alone at the age of 18, I learned how to be an efficient traveler and it helped make me very independent. Even now, my husband quite often says to me, "Okay, Ms. Independent."

ROASTED CHICKEN
with BLUEBERRY
PEPPERCORN SAUCE

BLUEBERRY
CORNBREAD
STUFFING

BRUSSEL SPROUTS

BLUEBERRY PUMPKIN
BARS

Roasted Chicken with Blueberry Peppercorn Sauce

Serves 4

1 roasted whole chicken
2 cloves garlic, minced
4 tablespoons butter

Preheat oven to 450°

Mix minced garlic and butter together in a small bowl. Take a sharp knife and cut back the skin of the chicken. Rub the inside of the chicken with the butter/garlic mixture. Roast chicken at 20 minutes per pound.

- -

Blueberry Peppercorn Sauce

For one 2lb roasted chicken, serves 4

¾ teaspoon peppercorn
½ cup white wine
½ cup chicken stock
4 teaspoons sugar
4 teaspoons butter
2 teaspoons balsamic vinegar
Salt to taste
¼ cup blueberries
3 teaspoons Blueberry Haven Blueberry Honey Mustard

In a saucepan, add sugar, wine, chicken stock, vinegar, peppercorns and blueberries. Stir until sugar is melted and mixed with the rest of the ingredients. Increase heat and add butter to thicken, do not let the sauce boil. Continue cooking until the liquid is reduced to half of what you started with.

Blueberry Cornbread Stuffing

Serves 6

1½ cups chopped onion
1 cup chopped celery
1 stick butter
½ lb ground pork sausage with sage
1 cup coarsely chopped mushrooms (I include some shitakes)
8 cups corn bread, crumbled (use 3 boxes Jiffy Corn Muffin
Mix or your favorite recipe)
2 teaspoons salt
1 teaspoon freshly ground peppercorns
1 ½ teaspoons poultry seasoning
½ teaspoon thyme
½ teaspoon rosemary
½ teaspoon nutmeg
1 cup white wine
1 egg, slightly beaten
1 cup Blueberry Haven Dried Blueberries

Sauté onions and celery until just tender and put in large
bowl. Cook sausage and mushrooms together. Pour off the
grease and add to celery and onion. Mix together with the
bread crumbs and seasonings. Just before stuffing the bird,
moisten mixture with the wine, add the egg and dried
blueberries, and mix well. Stuff the bird just before cooking.

Brussel Sprouts

Serves 4

4-5 cups Brussel sprouts
1 small shallot, minced
1 teaspoon garlic, minced
2 tablespoons balsamic vinegar
½ cup blueberries
4 oz goat cheese, crumbled
Salt and pepper

In a skillet, cook Brussel sprouts, shallots, and garlic. Sauté 3-4 minutes; the leaves on the Brussel sprouts will start to wilt. In a separate bowl, add all the above cooked ingredients. Add the vinegar and toss to combine. Add the blueberries and goat cheese and serve.

Blueberry Pumpkin Bars

Serves 6

4 eggs
1 2/3 cup sugar
1 cup vegetable oil
1 (15 oz) can pumpkin puree
2 cup all purpose flour
2 teaspoons baking powder
1 teaspoon baking soda
2 teaspoons cinnamon
½ cup Blueberry Haven Dried Blueberries
1 (4 oz pkg) cream cheese
½ cup butter, softened
1 teaspoon vanilla
2 cups powdered sugar

Preheat oven to 350°

In a medium bowl, mix the eggs, sugar, oil and pumpkin until light and fluffy. Sift together flour, baking powder, baking soda, and cinnamon. Stir dry mix into the pumpkin mixture until thoroughly combined. Add blueberries. Spread batter into 9"x13" pan. Bake 30-35 minutes. Cool before frosting.

Frosting
Cream together cream cheese and butter; stir in vanilla. Add powdered sugar, a little at a time. Spread on cooled bars. Cut into squares.

My Home Away From Home at Hope College

Hope College was a great experience, and I was once again in a whole new environment of people. I was one of very few Catholics on campus as Hope was affiliated with the Dutch Reformed Church. I had no clue what Dutch Reformed was or what it meant. Even though I had gone to Catholic schools, I had never been around people where religion was ever discussed. Although we may have known which church people attended, no one ever talked about their religious beliefs or let you know upon first meeting what churches they belonged to. I had always understood that religion was a private relationship between you and your god and was no one else's business.

It was at Hope College where I first saw someone praying in a public place -- the college dining hall. I was surprised at first, but when I looked around the room, everyone else was going about their business as if this was a normal activity. So I learned to do the same, and I now know to expect it when I am in public places in West Michigan.

Traveling and living with different cultures made me see what others knew and gave me a little more understanding of other cultures.

I laugh when people say, "Isn't Hope really religious?" Hope is a college experience like most other colleges. If you want to be really religious and go to chapel everyday and have religion as your major, you can. And the religion classes turned out to be some of my favorite. I enjoyed my history of religion classes, mostly because I had traveled to many of the places we spoke about. However, if I wanted to be in a sorority and drink beer at the local water holes, I could do that. One of the present watering holes in Holland, New Holland Brewery, was even started by a former Midland/Hope College student and he has grown into a fantastic microbrewer.

College was where I learned that life was a choice, and it was up to me to choose how life was going to affect me. I was in a sorority at Hope, and many of my closest friends today were my sorority sisters and friends at college. I even met my husband at Hope. He was raised in the greater Grand Rapids area in Rockford, one of the northern suburbs. Our kids are friends with our Hope College friends' children. Our kids have been coached by classmates we knew from Hope and played on multiple teams with Hope Alumni children. It's nice having that Hope College bond with so many people.

However, having raised our children in West Michigan, I will encourage them to leave this area for their own growth for college. I now value many of the experiences I had in life that helped me understand that other views and lifestyles are important.

HAVEN STUFFED PANCAKES

BLUEBERRY SMOOTHIE

Haven Stuffed Pancakes

Serves 2

3 eggs
½ cup milk
1 teaspoon vanilla
½ cup flour
Pinch of salt
⅛ teaspoon cinnamon
1 tablespoon sugar
2 tablespoons melted butter
Powdered sugar

Preheat oven to 400° and place 9" cast iron pan inside oven.

Mix together eggs, milk and vanilla. Sift in flour, salt, cinnamon and sugar until there are no lumps. Remove cast iron pan from oven and add butter until bottom of pan is completely coated. Pour batter into hot skillet.

Sprinkle with blueberries and place into heated oven; bake 15-20 minutes.

Blueberry Smoothie

Serves 1

1 cup fresh blueberries
1 cup Greek yogurt, vanilla flavored
½ cup skim milk
Handful of Ice

In a glass, add all ingredients together and mix; or place all ingredients in a blender and blend. Pour in a glass and top with a few fresh blueberries.

Summers at the Homestead

In the summer of 1985, the Brown family started a new summer tradition. With the grandparents deceased and families moving away from Maine, my parents bought a summer place in Glen Arbor, Michigan. The beautiful, little town of Glen Arbor on the Leelanau Peninsula is definitely a place in Michigan you don't want to miss. It is home to Lake Michigan, Sleeping Bear Dunes, many cottage people and fudgies. There is a difference between a cottage person and a fudgie. Fudgies are tourists who just visit Northern Michigan for a short period of time. Cottage (or summer) people own homes in the area, but they aren't locals as they don't live there year round. Since my family had no home anywhere else, we chose to spend our summers in Glen Arbor, and we were considered summer people. Most of the summer people were from downstate in Michigan, the Chicago area, or even Ohio and Indiana. We loved Glen Arbor as much as we had loved Cold Stream. In fact, the two are similar in many ways -- the cold fresh water, the heavy scent of pine trees and the great outdoors. The year my parents bought the place Up North, I had finished my freshman year in college, Katie had finished her freshman year in high school at the American School of Japan, and Giffie had finished fifth grade at the American School of Japan.

While Katie and I worked at the Homestead Resort or the many different restaurants during the summers, Giffie had free roam of all that Glen Arbor had to offer. He made the best of it. One day he and his buddy thought they would paddle their rubber raft from the Homestead to Sleeping Bear Dunes. I believe it was more than a 15-mile paddle, but I guess if you're in fifth grade it doesn't look too far. In a two-person, inflatable rubber dingy, the two 11-year-olds made a very dumb decision. But that wasn't the only time my mom had to call the Coast Guard for Giffie. There was another time when he was a little older and tried to windsurf from the Homestead to Little Manitou Island. The Homestead to Little Manitou Island in a speed boat takes over an hour. I think Katie or I had a boyfriend at that time who had a speed boat and they went out to 'rescue' Giffie. He was always finding adventures and fun everywhere he went in Glen Arbor.

Lake Michigan and its abundance of fresh water was great for freshwater fishing, so instead of lobster being the meat of choice, Up North it was Lake Michigan White Fish, a very mild tasting, white, flaky fish. Yum! There were no clams in Lake Michigan, just zebra mussels, an invasive species of the Great Lakes that hook onto the bottom of boats and freighters, like algae.

The Northern area of Michigan is known for being the Cherry Capital of the World, and much of the Up North industry revolves around cherry production. All over Northern Michigan are beautiful cherry trees, but not very many blueberries.

The other large industry in Northern Michigan is tourism. So, for summer jobs during college, I worked in the hospitality industry, like most of the summer kids and many local kids. We all waited on the many fudgies who visited Northern Michigan during the summers. In fact, my brother, sister and I worked at many different spots all over Glen Arbor -- The Soda Shop, La Becasse, The Totem Shop, as well as many different restaurants located within the Homestead properties. We worked as waiters, waitresses, bussers, newspaper deliverers, cashiers and dishwashers. My sister Katie even helped run a kids' day camp one summer, when her co-camp counselor took a break from the camp to start selling cherry-themed t-shirts out of the trunk of his car. Today that cherry company has multiple stores throughout the state of Michigan, carrying only cherry products. He has had great success, and it is awesome to see a local kid with a great idea turn it into a great Michigan company.

Working in the hospitality industry was a great job for any high school or college student. I learned great communication skills, as well as learning a lot about different types of people. The more I paid attention to the people I was serving and what their dislikes and likes were, the more it helped me in dealing with people. Little did I understand at the time how much it was going to affect my future.

WHITE FISH
TACOS

BLUEBERRY
POUND CAKE

White Fish Tacos

Serves 4

Blackened Seasoning:
2 teaspoons sea salt
1 teaspoon celery seed
1 tablespoon granulated sugar
1 tablespoon granulated garlic
1 tablespoon onion powder
1 tablespoon dried thyme
1 tablespoon dried oregano
1 tablespoon hot paprika
2 teaspoons freshly ground black pepper
2 teaspoons white pepper
1 teaspoon sweet paprika

Combine all ingredients and store in an airtight container.

12 pieces of bacon

In a large skillet over medium heat, cook bacon until browned and slightly crispy. Remove from heat, and place on paper towels to remove excess grease.

To Prepare Whitefish
Makes 4 servings

2 pounds whitefish, cleaned and patted dry
2 tablespoons blackened seasoning
2 tablespoons bacon grease (optional)

Toppings and Variations:
1 small red onion, sliced
1 cup cilantro, cleaned and roughly chopped
1 avocado, pitted and sliced
Blueberry Haven Blueberry Chutney
Blueberry Haven Blueberry Salsa

Toss whitefish with blackened seasoning to coat. Add bacon grease to a medium-size skillet over medium heat. Add whitefish to skillet and cook without disturbing, 3 minutes. Flip the fish and cook on the second side for 2-3 minutes more. Remove to a plate and let rest for a few minutes. Shred the fish into bite-sized pieces with two forks.

Place whitefish on each corn tortilla; add 1 slice of bacon (if you'd like), avocado, a pinch or two of cilantro, a few slices of red onion and 1 tablespoon of Blueberry Haven Blueberry Chutney or Blueberry Haven Blueberry Salsa.

Blueberry Pound Cake

Serves 8

2 cups sugar
1 cup butter softened
1 teaspoon vanilla
4 eggs
3 cups flour
½ teaspoon baking powder
2 cups blueberries

Preheat oven to 325°

In a large bowl, mix sugar and butter until light and fluffy; add vanilla and beat in eggs one at a time. Mix together flour and baking powder and beat into creamed mixture. Carefully fold in blueberries. Bake in 10-inch tube pan for 1 hour and 15 minutes.

How to Pick Blueberries in College

One of my favorite treats in college was to mix sugar, butter and flour together. Most of the time my friends and I made it because we were bored, wanted something sweet to eat and were too lazy to go to a store. As college students, we created treats with what ingredients we had on hand. One time when we had mixed up the flour, butter, and sugar, we thought it would be nice to add something else to it. But, we needed something cheap.

"Let's go picking," my roommate said.

"What picking? Blueberry picking?" I said.

There were blueberry farms everywhere in Holland, Michigan. We could pick blueberries anywhere, and they were cheap. So we got up off our brown velour couches, loaded into Lisa's brown Pinto and went to find a blueberry field. We drove to the north side of Holland where we were sure to find many u-picks. We found a farm, went to the office and got white plastic buckets with a rope attached to tie them around our waists. Lisa (from Zeeland) was showing me and the other Lisa (from Columbus) how to tie the buckets. Zeeland Lisa had grown up on a farm, so she knew what she was doing, so Columbus Lisa and I watched and mimicked her. We looked at each other with our buckets tied on, started laughing hysterically and laughed all the way into the fields.

I was wondering what the heck we were going to do with these buckets around our waists. I had never picked blueberries like this before. I had only picked low-bush blueberries in Maine, and we used a rake low to the ground. The bushes were as tall or taller than I was, and the blueberries were at the same height as my arm. We just stood there, shook the branch into our buckets, and the big blueberries fell off the bush and into our buckets -- kerplunk, kerplunk, kerplunk. That was the sound we heard the whole time we were picking as the berries hit the bottom of the plastic bucket. We took our t-shirts off as we had our bikini tops on underneath, and we chatted and picked. We were accomplishing two things at one time -- getting cheap food and a tan.

Once we had filled our five pound buckets, we decided we had enough berries and headed back into the farm to pay. The owner of the farm took our buckets, weighed the amount of berries we had, and dumped all the berries into our own bowls and pots. Zeeland Lisa had advised us to grab bowls and pots from our college house to put the blueberries in. When we left the blueberry farm, the back seat of Lisa's Pinto was filled with sauce pans, roasting pans, Tupperware bowls and metal bowls filled with blueberries. We drove back to our off-campus house and loaded every shelf inside the fridge with blueberries. We then each grabbed a bowl full of blueberries and returned to the couch in our TV area. Of course, we hadn't given any thought to what we were going to do with all of those blueberries. So, we decided we would make some breads, cakes and other treats that we could take to our 'friends' house. Our 'friends' were a group of boys in the Arcadian Fraternity who lived behind us. That was enough of a reason to get the three of us baking away.

BLUEBERRY HAVEN STREUSEL BARS with LEMON FILLING

BLUEBERRY FRUIT PIZZA

Blueberry Haven Streusel Bars with Lemon Filling

Serves 6

3 cups all-purpose flour
1½ cups rolled oats (not quick oats)
1 1/3 cups packed light brown sugar
1 teaspoon salt
1 teaspoon baking powder
1 cup (2 sticks) unsalted butter, at room temperature
3 large eggs, separated
2 cans (14 oz cans) sweetened condensed milk
1 cup fresh lemon juice
2 teaspoons lemon zest
3½ cups blueberries at room temperature

Preheat oven to 350°

Line a 13"x9" metal baking pan with foil, leaving a slight overhang on both sides to lift out the bars. Spray the pan/foil with cooking spray.

Whisk the flour, oats, brown sugar, salt and baking powder together in a large bowl. Cut the butter into the dry ingredients completely, until the pieces of butter are not visible. Set aside and reserve 2 cups of these crumbs for the topping. Beat the egg whites with a fork until broken up and foamy. Add egg whites to the crumbs and mix. Transfer the mixture to the prepared pan and press to form an even layer of crust. Bake for about 10-12 minutes, or until the top starts to look dry.

Whisk the condensed milk, lemon juice, lemon zest, and egg yolks together in a medium bowl. Let stand for 5 minutes; the mixture will begin to thicken slightly.

When the crust has finished baking, transfer the pan to a wire rack and sprinkle the blueberries evenly over the hot crust. Drop spoonfuls of the lemon mixture over the blueberries, then spread the lemon mixture gently to distribute. Work carefully so you don't crush the berries. Bake until the lemon layer begins to form a shiny skin, about 7-8 minutes.

Sprinkle reserved crumbs over the lemon layer. Use all of the crumb mixture to cover the lemon layer completely. Bake for 25-30 minutes, or until the filling is bubbling at the edges and the streusel topping is golden brown.

Transfer the pan to a wire rack and let the bars cool. Cut into squares before serving. The bars should be stored in the refrigerator.

Blueberry Fruit Pizza

Serves 6

1 refrigerated pie crust
½ cup butter, softened
1 cup flour
1 pint blueberries
1 cup sugar
Cinnamon to taste

Preheat oven to 350°

Lay out the pizza crust evenly on a pizza sheet or stone. Crimp the edges to make a rim. Sprinkle the pie crust with the blueberries.

In a bowl, mix butter, flour and sugar until it forms a crumbly mixture. Sprinkle the crumble onto the blueberries, then sprinkle with cinnamon. Bake at 350° for 45 minutes or until crust is nice and brown. Cool before serving.

Steve's Scoping Spot

The story of how I met my husband (Steve) is that he stalked me, starting the beginning of my freshman year at Hope. He says he didn't, but he did. He first picked out my picture in the Felicitations Book, which was a photo booklet put out of all the incoming new students. Most of the upperclassmen used this as a way to scope out the new, hot girls on campus. It was a kind of like Facebook before Facebook even existed.

Steve then noticed me in person at the ATM machine getting money when I was with my high school boyfriend. He would always position himself across from me in the Hope dining cafeteria. His fraternity had the best 'scoping spot' in the whole cafeteria, because their table was positioned against a brick wall. If they sat with their backs against the brick, they could see everyone in the cafeteria. Later his friends told me that when I would come in, if he wasn't directly across from me, he would get someone to trade seats with him. I never noticed and didn't officially meet him until the end of my freshman year.

On the last day of school, the sorority I had joined had a mixer with Steve's fraternity. I guess I was introduced to him that night, but I didn't stay at the party long as a bunch of my friends left the mixer to go to a party with the football players. The next day, one of my older sorority sisters asked if I would go out with him.

"Who? I don't know what guy he even was," I said.

"Stanley," she said.

"I don't remember meeting a Stanley. I met a guy who said his name was Steve."

"Yeah, that's Stanley," she said.

"Oh, ok." So I thought his name was Steve Stanley, since I knew a kid in high school whose last name was Stanley.

I was still kind of dating my high school boyfriend, but since spring break our relationship was not so great. All through our freshman year in college, we had grown apart and wanted different things out of life.

During his freshman and sophomore years, Steve had dated quite a few girls and always had a different girlfriend. He had even dated one of my girlfriends for a little while, and she was devastated when they broke up. The two of them were a perfect Dutch match, as were many of the other girls he dated. They came from Dutch heritage families and attended a CRC or Reformed Church. So, I told my sorority sister that I would go on one date with him, but I wasn't going to be just another one he dated.

Steve had already moved his belongings back home to Rockford, Michigan, for the summer. Rockford is a suburb north of Grand Rapids. Our first date was all arranged by his great buddy Scott, who was going to live and work in Holland for the summer. Scott made reservations for me and Steve at a great well-known Holland establishment called The Hatch. Since Steve was living at home, he was also able to drive one of his father's awesome cars to pick me up. The car was a brand new Corvette, which had recently come out with the new body style. I was impressed. Cars were always something that Steve's father enjoyed, and to this day he is driving one of the coolest cars in West Michigan. I would later find out that Steve's family owned a small family business in Grand Rapids, and at the time, much of the business revolved around the Michigan automotive industry.

Steve and I had a great time and I really enjoyed being with him. The day after our date, I was leaving to go to Midland, as my father was in from Tokyo on business and we were to fly to Tokyo together. I was going to work at The Key West Club, a Japanese restaurant, for the following six weeks. At the restaurant, I was to be the token guigen, Japanese slang for 'one with round eyes.' That meant Steve and I wouldn't see each other until the start of school in the fall, or so I thought.

The day after our first date, Steve sent a dozen roses to the Midland hotel where I was staying. I thought I might actually like this guy a little more than one date. Since I was going to be gone for the summer, I didn't think we would be in contact; however we kept in very close touch when I was in Tokyo, by phone and through many letters. When I came back and was living at the condo in Glen Arbor, he visited me on several different occasions -- again showing up in a different, cool car, as his dad had won a new black Camaro Z-28 in a car raffle. I was really starting to like him.

My mom wasn't so sure what to think about this kid and I can remember saying, "You'll be sorry you said that when I'm married to him."

I spent that summer dating a few different guys. In Tokyo, I met an American guy who went to NYU, and I went on a couple of dates with him. I also went on a disastrous date with the older brother of my sister's friend. Up at the Homestead, I met one of the tennis pros who had just graduated from college and I liked him a lot. Plus, I still hadn't quite broken it off with my high school boyfriend, and I also kept running into a Midland High guy whenever I was in Midland. So that summer was a lot of fun and very eventful for a girl who had dated the same boy for the past three years. I was having fun playing the field.

When I returned to Hope in the fall of 1985, Steve and I made our relationship more official after we were in an accident together. I had stopped at his house after my last hour of class. He and his fraternity brothers were hanging out on their back porch, which was a second story porch that was really part of the roof. He and I were joking around with one another, and I was telling him that I was going to a Tigers game with the tennis pro from the Homestead that weekend. The tennis pro was from Grand Rapids, and I wasn't sure I was ready to give him up yet. Steve pulled me down onto his lap as he was sitting in his rolling desk chair, and off the back end of the porch we went. He landed right in the chair, and I landed on my right arm. He felt responsible for my broken arm and took care of me and the hassles I had to deal with as a result of the broken arm. I always joked with him that once my cast came off, he'd give me a pink slip. The day my cast came off, he showed up in my college room with flowers and a pink slip saying, Are we still dating? I really, really liked him by that time. We dated on and off the rest of the time in college, mostly together, but we had a few typical college romance breakups. We did struggle through a period of time when we both wanted our independence from one another. It helped that Steve had graduated the year before me and was working in the Grand Rapids area during my senior year.

During the first semester of my senior year at Hope College, I did an off campus study in Philadelphia, Pennsylvania. I came back second semester and graduated with a communications degree. Steve made a trip out to Philadelphia to see me, along with a good college friend and his wife who had graduated from Hope. Scott and Paula (Scott had made our first date arrangements) were living and working in the metro New York area. They had gotten married within the last year.

CHICKEN
BLUEBERRY
CHUTNEY SALAD

BLUEBERRY
JALAPENO CORN
BREAD

Chicken Blueberry Chutney Salad

Serves 4

2 packages chicken tenderloins, cooked
1 cup Blueberry Haven Dried Blueberries
½ cup of slivered almonds
½ cup mayo
¼ cup Greek plain yogurt
1 tablespoon juice of freshly squeezed lemon
¼ cup Blueberry Haven Blueberry Chutney
Little salt and cracked pepper to taste
Romaine lettuce

Mix the mayo, yogurt, lemon juice and chutney together to make the dressing. Mix the chicken and almonds in the bowl with the dressing. With an ice cream scooper, scoop out the chicken and dressing mixture onto leaves of lettuce. I like to lay 2 pieces of romaine lettuce on the plate and put the chicken salad on top of the lettuce. Sprinkle with blueberries, and flavor each with a little salt and cracked pepper.

Blueberry Jalapeno Corn Bread

Serves 4

1 cup all purpose flour
3/4 cup corn meal
3 tablespoons granulated sugar
2 teaspoons baking powder
3/4 teaspoon salt
1 egg
2/3 cup milk
1/3 cup light olive oil
1 cup fresh blueberries
1 small can green chilies
2 slices Havarti cheese

Preheat oven to 350°

Mix together flour, corn meal, sugar, baking powder and salt
in a large bowl. In a smaller bowl, mix together egg, milk and
olive oil. Pour the liquid mixture into the flour mixture.
Fold in the blueberries and chilies. Pour into a lightly
greased 8"x8" pan. Add the two slices of Havarti on top.
Bake at 350° for about 30 minutes, or until a toothpick
comes out clean.

Working My Way Through Philly

I graduated from Hope College in the spring of 1988 with a communications degree, and thought I would work in a public relations firm or an ad agency similar to my off campus internship in Philadelphia.

During my internship, I lived with five of my sorority sisters who were also on the off campus semester. We had so much fun. We walked everywhere and lived just a couple of blocks from the Liberty Bell. Every day on my way to work I walked by the bell, and I loved it.

The public relations agency I worked in was an eye opening-experience for me. The firm was owned by two African American woman, Yvonne and Francine, and most of their work was done for Mayor Good, the mayor of Philadelphia at the time. I still remember that I would come home from work and tell my roommates what the two woman had done that day. Every day at work the women would start with, "Now, girlfriend," and "I need to tell you," and they would go into some story that had me in stitches. I was out of my element with projects and events the agency had, and I was often the "you white girl" at all the events.

After I graduated from Hope, I had a few jobs. One was with a Grand Rapids concert venue promoter, and I also worked part-time at a department store. While I was working these jobs, I received a call from Job Placement at Hope College. They wanted me to attend an interview at a women's clothing store chain with 284 stores headquartered in Grand Rapids. The Gantos Corporation was looking for buyer/management trainees, and I thought it sounded interesting. By the time I got out of college, I had realized that taste was not something taught -- you either had it or you didn't. I was lucky enough to have gotten it from my mother. She can put on a dress from Target, go to a million dollar wedding in New York City, and pull off the best dressed.

I went through a process of interviews at the Gantos corporate offices and was offered a position in the management/buyer training program. I didn't know it at the time, but everything I was about to learn at the Gantos School of Retail, I would use to one day start my own company.

During this time, there were no management training positions available in the Midwest, and I wasn't interested in being a store manager. Since I have always been more creative and talented at picking out trends, I wanted to be in the buying department; however, to get into the buyer part of the training program, I had to go through the store manager training first. The Gantos chain had been expanding all across the United States, and the most recent store expansion was in the New England area. Since I was born a New Englander and had lived there the first part of my life, I thought it sounded great. Plus, I still had cousins living in New England. I was offered a choice of three cities: Danbury, Connecticut; Poughkeepsie, New York; or the Boston area. It was not a hard choice for me -- I chose Boston, because my dad had attended college in Boston. My dad went to Bentley College, located in downtown Boston on Boylston Street. I had lived in Boston with my mom and dad while he was finishing up his accounting degree.

The store I was training at was located in Nashua, New Hampshire, about 40 minutes from downtown Boston. There was also a store at Copley Place in downtown Boston that I might be working at occasionally, and I started working at Pheasant Lane Mall in Nashua right after Labor Day. I loved being back in New England, and I could still understand everything the New Englanders said.

I rented my first apartment in downtown Nashua. It was a little studio apartment in an older building owned by the soon-to-be Governor of New Hampshire, Judd Greg.

The store had a store manager, an assistant manager, and two management trainees who worked full-time. There was also a staff of part-time workers, and I learned a lot from the sales ladies -- JoAnn in sportswear and Norma in dresses -- who worked at the store. They were both professional sales women and they could sell. The dress business at Gantos was a very large business and one of its most profitable, I would later learn. They led the industry in special event and daytime dresses.

Norma could sell a dress to anyone and convince the customer that it was perfect for them. She outfitted many mothers of brides and grooms -- "mobs" and "gobs" -- as she called them. Norma was over 70 and always had perfect red fingernails and red lipstick.

Leslie, the assistant manager of the store, and I became came quick friends. She had graduated from Ohio University the year before, so we were close in age. We became partners in crime in the Boston night life. Not actually Boston, because she lived in Newton, MA, right outside the city where Boston College is located. Most weekends we spent together frequenting different spots in Newton. We didn't get much time off at the same time, but when we did, we took full advantage of having a great time together.

On occasion, I dated a guy that Leslie and I met one night when we were out in Boston. I was still in touch with Steve, who was living in Grand Rapids. We talked on the phone as he was busy working and I'm sure playing the field as I was.

The Gantos program was a fantastic training program, and it was there that I learned how to run a retail store. I learned every aspect of the store, including how to be a sales person, a utility person, a window dresser, set up the store layout, check in merchandise and watch the sales figures: weekly, daily and hourly. It was great hands-on experience. Typically, when a trainee graduated from the management training program, she was (hopefully) promoted to assistant manager of a store. I finished the training program in January and was offered an assistant store manager position in a new store opening in the Upstate New York area. So, after only six months in Nashua, I was packing up my belongings and relocating. All that moving during my childhood was coming in handy.

SALMON AND BLUEBERRY CHERRY TOMATO CROSTINI

MACATAWA BLUEBERRY CAKE

BRIE and BLUEBERRY HAVEN CHUTNEY

Salmon and Blueberry
Cherry Tomato Crostini

Serves 4

2 cups fresh blueberries
1 cup cherry tomatoes, cut in half
1 cup chopped fresh chives
1 tablespoon chopped fresh parsley
1 tablespoon balsamic vinegar
1 teaspoon fresh lemon juice
A little light olive oil and Blueberry Haven Blossom Honey
1 French baguette
Salt and Pepper to taste
1 salmon fillet
Blueberry Haven Blueberry Honey Mustard

Preheat oven to 350°

In a bowl, mix blueberries, cherry tomatoes, chives, parsley, vinegar, and lemon juice, and drizzle with a little olive oil and blueberry honey. Add salt and pepper to taste. Set the bowl in the refrigerator.

Thinly slice baguette and lightly coat each side of bread with olive oil. Bake on a cookie sheet at 350° for 15-20 minutes.

On another cookie sheet lined with tin foil, place the salmon fillet, and lightly coat one side with olive oil, salt and pepper. On the other side of the fillet, spread the Blueberry Haven Blueberry Honey Mustard. Bake the fillet for 25-30 minutes, until it pulls apart easily with a fork.

Top the crostini with the salmon and blueberry cherry tomatoes. Sprinkle with parsley and a little cracked pepper.

Macatawa
Blueberry Cake

Serves 4

1 large box of fresh blueberries
1 stick of butter
1 cup of sugar
3 eggs (jumbo or large)
¾ cup flour

Preheat oven to 350°

Cream butter and sugar together. Add eggs one at a time.
Add dry ingredients and beat together. Mix well; the
mixture will be thick. Pour into a greased 9"x9" pan. Press
the berries lightly on top of the batter. Bake at 350° for 40
minutes.

Serve with real whipped cream. We like to fold a little of
Blueberry Haven's Blueberry Elixir into the fresh cream.

Brie and Blueberry Haven Chutney

Serves 4

1 round of brie or your favorite soft cheese, like goat or cream cheese
1 jar of Blueberry Haven Blueberry Chutney
Water crackers

Spoon Blueberry Haven Blueberry Chutney into the center of the wheel of brie.

Serve with water crackers.

Will You Marry Me?

The new Gantos store in Rotterdam Square Mall in Schenectady, New York, just outside Albany, was my next destination. It didn't take me long to discover that I wasn't going to get into the buyer training program as quickly as I had anticipated. It was a competitive job to obtain, and I needed to be working in store management for at least a year.

I moved into a small condo about five minutes away from the mall, worked and learned a great deal. The manager, Deanna, who had come from another Gantos store on Long Island, and I were to head up this brand new store. When we got there, the store was an empty shell. There was no merchandise, staff or anything. So Deanna and I, along with our district manager, went to work. We interviewed and hired staff, received and set up merchandise, dressed the window, and got the store ready for its grand opening. This was a big deal, and all the bigwigs from Grand Rapids were flying out to cut the ribbon and open the store. I was very nervous on the day Mr. Gantos and the President of Store Operations were coming to our store. I had heard stories about L. Douglas Gantos, and how he was big, loud, and had very high standards and expectations. I was 22, fresh out of college and eager to make an impression.

The day of the grand opening came and everything was perfect. We had balloons and refreshments, and our store looked great. Deanna and I were even photographed with Mr. Gantos and the President of Store Operations, and our picture was in the local Schenectady paper. Our store was doing well with sales, and we were hiring and training new staff. We had two ladies who were management trainees working with me and Deanna.

I spent my free time with the trainees and would go to Connecticut quite often, where Columbus Lisa was living with her boyfriend. They lived in a beachfront town called Old Saybrook, and in the summer it was a lot of fun to hang out with them and their friends. It didn't help that I had taken to liking one of her husband's friends, Dennis. Steve and I had never really said to each other that we were seeing other people, but it was an unspoken agreement while we were dating long distance. He hadn't been out to visit me since I had moved to the New England area.

For the 4th of July holiday, I had decided to go home to Glen Arbor to take some time off from work. I hadn't seen my family or Steve since leaving the past September when I had moved to Nashua. Steve asked me to fly into Grand Rapids so he and I could go to Mackinac Island for some alone time before we headed up to my parents' house for the long weekend. I thought that maybe he was sick of being apart, so he was going to ask me to marry him on Mackinac I also thought it was awesome that he had planned something special.

Before I left Nashua, I had decided (and told Columbus Lisa), that if Steve and I weren't engaged by the end of the weekend, it would be time to end it. The long distance relationship was taking its toll. I knew I loved him, but I hadn't seen him in so long, as he hadn't visited.

Steve picked me up at the airport and we drove to Mackinaw City. As we left the airport in Grand Rapids, we drove by the Gantos Headquarters. It was an impressive building with an all-glass front, and as we drove by I could see the lobby. Inside the lobby was a huge, two-sided marble staircase that led to the upstairs, a marble receptionist desk, and the ever-famous Gantos lady that was made out of fluorescent lighting adorning the top of the staircase. As we drove by, I thought to myself that I just want to work in that office.

We got to Mackinaw City about mid-afternoon and took the ferry across to Mackinac Island. Our drive to Mackinaw City had been great, and we talked the entire time about work, what we were doing, and how great our future together was going to be. I was thinking, I'm getting a ring, I'm getting a ring. Once on the island, we rode bikes around the island, talked, laughed and had dinner (with more talking and laughing). We were having a great time, and I thought there were many perfect opportunities for Steve to give me a ring -- but nothing. We caught the ferry back to Mackinaw City and made the two-hour drive to Glen Arbor and arrived at the condo at about midnight. My parents were waiting up for us, my sister was back from working in one of the local restaurants, and Giffie was asleep in the room with the twin beds where Steve would be sleeping.

The next day was my Mom's birthday, and we had a big family dinner planned at one of her favorite restaurants. Steve and I were going into town for coffee, and then we were going to meet everyone at the beach. I was thinking that since we were going to be alone again…maybe? But, no. We got our coffees and went straight to the beach where we spent the entire day reading and hanging out. As we started to head back, my dad said that he was going to the store and Steve offered to go with him. What I didn't know was that earlier in the week, Steve had been trying to reach my dad, but they never connected. At that time, my dad still worked for Dow Corning, although now he had more responsibilities and was often in meetings, traveling, and hard to reach.

Mom, Giffie, and I headed back to the condo to get ready for dinner, talking about all the great things that were on the menu and what we were going to have for dinner. We had to take two cars into Traverse City for dinner, and since Giffie had just gotten his learner's permit, he asked if he could come with Steve and me so he could drive. I said that was fine. Mom, Katie and I got ready, and my dad and Steve were still not back from the store.

"Where the heck did they go to get beer," I asked. "Crystal Lake," my mom said. Crystal Lake was about an hour from Glen Arbor, and it shouldn't have taken them that long. The two of them got back in time to take five-minute showers before we had to leave for the restaurant. I told Steve that Giffie was going to ride with us. Steve gave me an odd look, pulled me aside and said, "I don't want your brother going with us. I don't want him driving my car."

I was thinking, What a jerk and seriously, what's the big deal? You have a Chevy Cavalier -- get over yourself. We all left the condo at the same time and headed to the restaurant. As we got into the car, my dad said, "We'll see you when you get there." Steve smiled at him, and I was thinking, "Whatever."

We drove through the town of Leland to get to Traverse City, and Steve suggested that we stop at Fishtown and have a drink outside on the patio at a restaurant named The Cove. At this point, I was just going with it. Nothing all weekend had gone as I had planned. We sat at a small table right along the river, near a dam of churning water. As we sat down and ordered, a boat, obviously not familiar with Leland, started coming into this river area, and it was driving right toward the dam. I was looking at Steve, the boat and all the other people looking at the boat, wondering what the heck they were doing and how they were going to turn around. At the last minute, the boater realized what was going on, stopped the boat and reversed it out of the channel. As the chaos settled down, I turned back around to the table and sitting in front of me was a box. I looked at Steve and put my hand on the box. He got down on one knee and said, "Before you open that, will you marry me?" Now I was crying, and everyone in the restaurant was clapping. I opened the box, slipped on the ring and said, "Yes." I was soooo happy and couldn't believe it had finally happened. After dating for four years, we were going to get married.

After we left The Cove in Leland, we drove to Traverse City to meet my family. On the way there, Steve explained that he wanted to ask me in Mackinac but couldn't reach my dad to ask his permission. Then when I told him that Giffie wanted to come with us, he knew he had to pull a jerk stunt. Now it all made sense! We got to the restaurant, and my parents had smiles on their faces and champagne waiting for us. Katie and Giffie were laughing about how Steve said Giffie couldn't come with us and how they knew I was ticked. They all had a good chuckle and said good luck to Steve, since he was going to have to put up with me the rest of his life.

"This isn't Nordstrom," my dad warned him. "You asked for her and there are no returns."

GRILLED BLUEBERRY PORK TENDERLOINS

SHIRLEY'S MASHED POTATOES

ROASTED ASPARAGUS

WHITE CHOCOLATE TART with BLUEBERRIES

Grilled Blueberry Pork Tenderloins

Serves 4

¾ to 1 lb pork tenderloin
2 medium red onions
¼ cup cabernet sauvignon -- my favorite is Hess
1 cup cherry tomatoes
1 cup blueberries
2 tablespoons butter
Little cracked pepper
Little salt
2 teaspoons balsamic vinegar
2 teaspoons sugar

Grill pork, turning occasionally, until cooked, about 20 minutes. Keep warm in the oven in tin foil. In a large sauce pan, melt the butter and add onions; season with salt and pepper. Cook until golden brown, about 10 minutes. Add sugar and cook until the onions are caramelized; watch closely for about 3 minutes more. Add wine, vinegar, blueberries and cherry tomatoes. Bring to a boil and remove from heat. Thinly slice pork and serve with sauce.

If you are in a hurry and don't have time to make the sauce, pick up a jar of Blueberry Haven Blueberry Chutney. Pour the sauce in a saucepan and heat thoroughly; serve. Perfect meal complements are Michigan grilled asparagus and mashed potatoes.

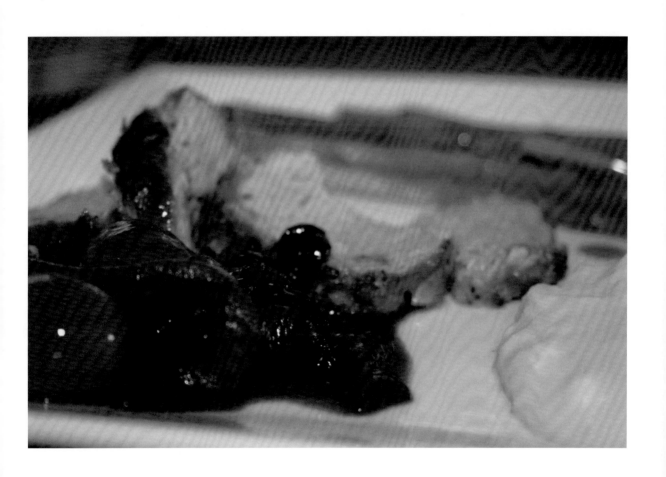

Shirley's Mashed Potatoes
(better than mine, my kids say)

Serves 4

4 cups mashed potatoes
2 cups cottage cheese
¾ cup sour cream
1 teaspoon salt
2 tablespoons butter, melted

Preheat oven to 350°

In a bowl, combine potatoes, cottage cheese, sour cream,
salt and pepper. Transfer to a greased 2-qt. baking dish.
Drizzle with butter. Bake, uncovered, at 350° for 30 minutes,
then cover with tin foil and bake 5 minutes longer or until
heated through.

Roasted Asparagus

Serves 4

2 lbs of asparagus
Olive oil
Salt and pepper to taste
Butter, melted
Onion
Garlic

Spray a cookie sheet with cooking spray and set aside.

Preheat oven to 350°.

In a bowl, mix the tips of about half of the asparagus with olive oil and salt and pepper. Spread on cookie sheet and roast about 5-7 minutes.

In a separate bowl mix melted butter with chopped onion and garlic. After asparagus is grilled, drizzle butter mixture on top and serve immediately.

White Chocolate Tart with Blueberries

Serves 4

1 2/3 cups graham cracker crumbs
1/3 cups, unsalted butter, melted
6 squares white chocolate
2/3 cup whipping cream
2 tablespoons unsalted butter, at room temperature and cut into small pieces
1 lemon
2 cups blueberries

Preheat oven to 350°

In a medium bowl, combine graham cracker crumbs and melted butter. Press into the sides of a tart pan. Bake for 8-10 minutes until crust is brown; set aside and let cool. Zest the lemon over the entire baked crust.

Put chocolate in a bowl. In a small saucepan, heat the cream until just boiling and pour over the chocolate. Let sit for about 2 minutes and then whisk until completely smooth; add butter and keep whisking. Pour the chocolate mixture into the warm crust. Chill overnight and top with berries just before serving.

Moving Back to
West Michigan

I moved back to the Grand Rapids area in September of 1989, almost a year to the date when I had left for New England. I was lucky Gantos had an opening at one of the stores in that area, and I was to be the assistant manager at City Center, located in downtown Grand Rapids. It was the perfect location as Steve and I had bought a house on the northeast side of Grand Rapids, and I was living there by myself until we were married. Our wedding was set for May of 1990. It didn't take

me long to re-acclimate to West Michigan. I had a lot to do with a new job, planning a wedding, and being with Steve full time after being apart for a year. I enjoyed working at the Gantos downtown, but was still hoping to get into the buyer training program. It was a coveted program that many of the girls in the stores wanted to get into. It was where you worked in the corporate office, and were taught how to buy and develop product. Very few people got into the buying program.

I had been in management for over a year now and had no interest in managing more Gantos stores. Plus, the Gantos market in Grand Rapids was very saturated with Gantos employees who would want that same job in the area. I was constantly bothering my district and store managers for information on when the next round of interviews for the program would occur. They usually rolled their eyes at me and told me I had no chance of getting into it. My district manager had been with Gantos for years in the same position. My store manager had been a store manager and worked for Gantos much longer then I had. I worked hard, tried to stay out of her way, and just got my job done. At that time there were four Gantos stores in Grand Rapids, two in Kalamazoo and one in Muskegon. The next closest Gantos stores were in Lansing, so there was a lot of competition for positions. Since I was one of the last employees hired, I was low on the list.

In February of 1990, interviewing would begin for the new class of buyer trainees. Over 100 applicants from the stores had expressed interest in applying. Girls from all over the United States were applying to get the five spots available. There were positions in sportswear, accessories, jewelry, dresses, and coats. We had met many of the buyer trainees from the previous classes, because they were often doing walk-throughs in the local stores to see what their merchandise looked like. A walk-though was done weekly in buying offices, mostly on Friday mornings. They walked around the store to make sure the merchandise was placed in the direction the buyer had wanted and that the store had a flow to keep the customer shopping throughout the entire store. In the buying class that was getting ready to 'graduate,' there were girls from Long Island, New Hampshire, Missouri, Minnesota, and one from the Grand Rapids area.

The interview, as I discovered, was a full day process in which we would meet with a buyer, someone from human resources, the vice president of human resources, a merchandise manager, and a planning manager. We would then take a math test. I hadn't had a math class since high school and hadn't taken any math at Hope College. It was the one area on my ACT where I had scored high enough so I didn't have to take any math classes if I wasn't in a math field. I had no clue what I was getting myself into with this interview process.

I had been in the corporate offices before but never in the work spaces. There were busy people moving quickly in the rows and rows of desks, with lots of chatter, people on the phones, racks of clothes everywhere and the smell of several women's perfumes. With all those clothes everywhere and so many people with a great sense of fashion,

I thought I had died and gone to heaven.

My first interview was with Danette Palazallo, the buyer. She was very intimidating. She shot question after question at me, looking at me over little spectacles perched on her nose. She asked questions like, "Why do you want this job?" and "What do you have to offer?" The interviews went on like that all day from person to person. I would later find out from my district and store managers that I had interviewed with the sportswear buyer and sportswear merchandise manager. The two of them were known to be the toughest interviewers, with very high standards and strong opinions. I thought, *Great, I'll never get picked.* There were 10 of us there that day interviewing, with only five positions available. I didn't meet all 9 of the other candidates, but I did meet a couple. One was Laura and she was impeccably dressed, with red lipstick that matched her outfit. She was working in the corporate office in the planning end and had worked at Jacobson's, a well known Michigan department store. I also met Kelly, who was from the Indianapolis store, which was one of Gantos' best producing stores. Kelly was from Kentucky, was 5'8", and had a great accent and long, blonde hair. I saw other girls, but Kelly and Laura were who I remembered from that day as we took the math test together. After the round of interviews and the math test, we were sent on our way and told they would be 'in touch.'

I went back to working at City Centre and was reminded by my store manager (now pregnant) that there was no way I would get the job. I think she just liked to antagonize me and lower my self confidence by reminding me she was at a much higher-playing level than me.

LAURA'S BLISS
BLUEBERRY PUNCH

BAKED SALMON
WITH BLUEBERRY
SAUCE

CAYCE'S GRAHAM
CRACKER MINI PIES

Laura's Bliss Blueberry Punch

Serves 4

1 large can apricot nectar
1 large can pineapple juice
1 jar Blueberry Haven Blueberry Elixir
3 small cans of frozen limeade
2 liters of Canada Dry
Vodka, optional

Mix all ingredients and stir. Great for wedding and baby showers served in a punch bowl.

Baked Salmon with Blueberry Sauce

Serves 4

2 tablespoons butter
2 cloves garlic, minced
2 salmon fillets
½ lemon, juiced
1 tablespoon cornstarch
½ cup blueberries
2 tablespoons balsamic vinegar
1 tablespoon sugar
½ cup chicken broth
1 teaspoon fresh thyme
Salt and pepper

Preheat oven to 400°

Pat salmon dry. Mix together the butter and garlic, and spread on the salmon; season with salt and pepper.

In a small bowl, mix, lemon juice and cornstarch, and then pour into a small saucepan with the blueberries, balsamic vinegar, broth and thyme. Simmer on low for about 20-30 minutes; sauce will be reduced by about half. In a small sauté pan, heat a small amount of butter. Place salmon on pan, skin side down and cook for about 1-2 minutes, until flesh begins to turn pink. Remove from skillet and put in the oven for 7-8 minutes.

We enjoy this served with wild rice.

Cayce's Graham Cracker Mini Pies

Serves 8

Pre packaged mini graham cracker pie crusts
Instant vanilla pudding
Blueberry Haven Blueberry Topping
Cool Whip©
Fresh Blueberries

Follow the package instructions to make the instant
pudding. Scoop pudding into each pie crusts (about 8).
Cover the pudding with the Blueberry Haven Blueberry
Topping. Add a dollop of Cool Whip© and top with a couple
fresh blueberries. Put in refrigerator to cool and set.

Accepted Into the
Gantos Buying Program

At the end of April of 1990, my district manager showed up at the store unexpectedly one day. She pulled me into the back office and told me she had something to talk to me about. I was nervous and was afraid I had done something wrong. She closed the door to the office and was upbeat and friendly.

"You were accepted into the Buyer Training Program," she said.

"What?" I said. I was not sure I had heard her right.

She continued, "You are going to the corporate offices to work."

I couldn't believe it -- I was so happy. She told me how proud she was I had been accepted in the program, and she knew I was going to the get the job. She hugged me, then followed me into the store area as I told my store manager the good news. When I told her I got the job, the look on her face was total surprise, but she looked over at our district manager.

"Congratulations, that's great," she said as she hugged me. "When do you start?"

"I start on Monday, so I'll still have the weekend to finish out."

The last three days were great at City Center as everyone was happy for me, even my store manager. I would run across both my district manager and the store manager on and off over the next six years that I worked at the corporate offices. They would seem genuinely happy to introduce me to whomever was in the store, and always prefaced my introduction with, "This is the buyer we trained." I always smiled and went on my way, back to the corporate offices.

I started working at the offices located on Patterson Ave. in Kentwood, a southern suburb of Grand Rapids, exactly two weeks before Steve and I were to be married. Lucky for me, the buyer I was working for had just gotten married herself so she was very understanding. The first day of the program, all the buyer trainees were in one room, and as I walked in I was happy to see both Kelly, who would work in jewelry, and Laura, who would work in sportswear. The other two girls were Dawn, who would be in dresses, and Annette, would work in separates, sportswear and swimwear. I was assigned to accessories, which included belts, hats, scarves, handbags, gloves, gifts and fragrances. Teressa was the buyer I would be working for, and Sue was the merchandising manager who I would work under. Sue was in charge of jewelry, accessories, and lingerie, and she reported to the vice president of merchandising. We all, however, reported to L. Douglas Gantos. When you heard your name announced over the intercom and to dial extension 205, you jumped because you knew it meant Douglas was beckoning you.

Teressa and Sue taught me all they knew, and they knew a lot. Sue had risen from the warehouse in Gantos to her current position. She had never attended college, but she was one tough lady. Teressa was from the South and had come from a department store in the Nashville area. From Teressa, I learned how to negotiate using sugar. She knew how to work the southern charm, sweetness and good looks to get what she needed out of her vendors. Sue was a relentless negotiator and never took "no" for an answer.

Teressa and Sue were very different and often butted heads. As I would come to learn, that's what an office of all women was often like. However, we had a blast, worked hard (and a lot), and I loved just about every minute I worked at the Gantos Corporate offices. I started as the buyer trainee in accessories and then was promoted to the assistant buyer in accessories. From there I was promoted to dress buyer. At the time, I was 26 years old, and my dress department was a $38 million dollar department.

During my corporate time, I learned how to run a retail store from the back end, which included buying, planning, product development, advertising, and merchandising. It also included the costs of goods, markdowns, weeks of supplies, negotiating, liquidating merchandise, and private label merchandise. We traveled to New York City every month for a week of buying trips. Four times a year we traveled to Los Angeles for buying trips. There were also special trips for advertising and upper management, for trend shopping to great places like Italy and the south of France. Weeks in New York were a whirlwind. We would get to the offices on Sundays to pick up and go over our reports.

During our weekly trips to New York, we had vendor appointments from 8:00 a.m. until 6:00 p.m. Then we were often out for dinner and to shows at all the hot spots in New York until the wee hours of the morning. This would go on every day until Friday when we would fly back to Grand Rapids. There were many times when we worked on very little sleep and often with a pretty good hangover, but we worked hard and smart.

The people who were at Gantos with me during my years there have all gone on to be incredibly successful. Many have opened their own businesses around West Michigan, with many working in retail companies in West Michigan and around the country. We truly had the best training from the Gantos Corporation, as crazy, tough and fun as it was. Who knew that all that knowledge I learned in ten years in the Gantos stores and buying office would come in very handy when I started my own business?

LAMB CHOPS with BLUEBERRY RELISH

MA HOEK'S SPECIAL CREAM with BLUEBERRIES

Lamb Chops with Blueberry Relish

Serves 4

Blueberry Relish (see recipe below)
One cup fresh blueberries
Pinch of lemon zest from a fresh lemon
1 tablespoon fresh basil, rolled and chopped
2 teaspoons red onion chopped
1 tablespoon red wine vinegar
2 teaspoons red wine
1 teaspoon peppercorns
4 lamb chops
Light olive oil
Salt and pepper

Coat the bottom of a sauté pan in light olive oil. Heat the pan until it is really hot, almost smoking. Lower the heat to medium. Add the lamb to the pan and sear the lamb on all sides. Take the lamb out of the pan and let cool. Top with the Blueberry Relish.

Blueberry Relish:

In a bowl, mix together blueberries, lemon zest, basil, onion, red wine vinegar, and peppercorns. Cover and put in the fridge for at least one hour. You can make this several days ahead.

We love to serve this with fresh Michigan sweet corn and Michigan red potatoes.

Ma Hoek's Special Cream with Blueberries

Serves 6

1 cup sugar
2 cups heavy cream
1 teaspoon gelatin
2 cups sour cream
2 teaspoons vanilla
Fresh Blueberries or Blueberry Haven Topping

Combine sugar and gelatin in a double boiler and cook slowly for 10 minutes, or until sugar is dissolved. Let cool in pan for about 10-15 minutes. Whisk in sour cream and vanilla; put into bowls and let firm in the fridge. Top with fresh blueberries, Blueberry Haven Blueberry Topping, or any of our blueberry jams.

We're Getting Married

Steve and I were married on May 12, 1990. The ceremony took place at the Chapel at Western Seminary in Holland, Michigan, a quaint little chapel on the campus of Hope College. Steve's youth pastor, Pastor Dave, preformed the ceremony, and my sister Katie was my maid of honor. The two Lisas, (Columbus and Zeeland), my cousin Jill and my good friend Shelly were all in the wedding party. They looked so pretty in their pink dresses and pink flowers. Steve had his two brothers as his best men, and my brother Giffie, Steve's best high school buddy Dave, and his college buddy Scott, who had set up our first date, were the groomsmen. My dear friends and sorority sisters from Hope, Bobbi and Carolyn, served as Mistresses of Ceremonies.

It was a perfect May day in Michigan, with grey skies, a little rain,

a little snow, and of course, thunder and lightning. The weather was actually pretty amazing as we watched the lightning from the 26th floor of the Amway Grand Plaza Hotel in downtown Grand Rapids. Our reception was held in a room overlooking the city and the river, and the lightning was quite a sight with the glass windows that surrounded the 26th floor. Our reception was pretty much a giant cocktail party, and of course, we had wedding cake.

I'm not much of a cake person, so I asked the event

planner at the Amway Grand if we could have cheesecake instead of traditional wedding cake. She looked at me like I was a little strange but said she didn't see why not. So instead of a traditional wedding cake, we had cheesecake. It was delicious, and all the guests commented on how different it was.

Steve and I went to Hawaii on our honeymoon. We went to Kauai, which in my personal opinion, was the prettiest island. When we returned, we lived at our house on the northeast side of Grand Rapids. I continued to work at Gantos, and Steve was working as a financial planner. He was a business major at Hope College and loved the stock market. Later, he would join the family business of Hansen Balk Steel Treating. He joined the business after his father had a heart attack and was diagnosed with prostate cancer.

We were a typical, young married couple, working and hanging out with friends. We spent a lot of our free time with the girls I worked with at Gantos and their husbands. None of our friends had children for a while, and we were the couple who got a dog first. He was our first baby, a Chesapeake Bay Retriever named Sawyer. We had gone with friends to pick up their dog, and of course we came home with one, too. It was shortly after getting Sawyer that many of our friends starting getting pregnant.

Keegan, our first son, was born in February of 1995. I was still working at Gantos, and they offered day care at the corporate facility where I worked, so going back to work after having a baby was pretty easy. However, when I was out on maternity leave, my accessories work partner, Laura, the one with perfect lipstick, also had a baby. This was her second child, and she decided not to return to work with two children. Her daughter Tori and my son Keegan were only 10 days apart, and we had lots of fun together while I was on maternity leave.

I did have a rough time when I went back to work as my boss had been diagnosed with cancer, got pregnant and was going out on maternity leave. Before I had left for maternity leave, I was doing a lot of her job, because she couldn't travel and was not in the office. During that time, I spent a lot of time traveling with L. Douglas Gantos and his wife Kathy. She also had a daughter named Tiffany, and they would call me their

"Work T." I would also meet Douglas for dinner in New York when Kathy didn't travel with him, and I was not intimidated by him as much anymore. I learned that his gruffness was part of the charm of his personality. He was a big man who stood about 6'4", and I was now used to his big presence. He seemed to respect my opinion, and my humor.

"Tiffany you went to Michigan, right?" he said in a meeting one day.

"Douglas, if you say I went to Michigan, I went to Michigan," I said.

He also often complimented my sense of style and dress.

"Why can't we buy dresses for our store, like how you dress," he said on one occasion.

"Now that we are across the United States, the average customer will not pay what I pay for a dress," I said. "Our customer will only pay $79.99 for a dress."

Gantos, from the start, was a high-fashion store that carried high-end merchandise. As the chain got bigger, the masses of the United States were not high-end customers. Therefore, the price points of the merchandise needed to be lower.

While I was out on maternity leave, I believe Douglas might have glorified my dress department and my accomplishments to my boss, and when I came back, my dress department was in shambles. Before I went out on my leave, I was enjoying thirty-four percent to forty percent increases in dress sales, due to the fact that I was very good at scrambling for merchandise and was NEVER overstocked. When I returned, my department was overstocked with units from a vendor that I would never go to because I didn't like their product and I didn't care for the owner. He was also one of my boss' closest friends in the dress market. Therefore, when I returned to work, it didn't feel the same, and I didn't have the same passion. Plus, my boss, who was in charge of daytime dresses, evening dresses and coats was unbearable.

One morning I was walking in late because I had spent a few minutes talking to the daycare staff when I dropped Keegan off in the morning. They were so good to Keegan, and he was such an easy baby -- always happy and hardly ever crying. He would sit and play alone while the women dealt with the fussier kids. As I was walking up the beautiful marble steps to my third floor office, behind me was Douglas.

"You're late," he said in his gruff voice.

"Yeah, I am," I said. "I'm sorry."

"Honey, why are you doing this?" he asked.

I looked at him, hoping I wouldn't cry.

"I know your husband's family owns a business in this town and you don't need this job."

I looked at him, smiled and kept going up the steps.

Keegan was almost one at this time, and I had just gotten back from a New York buying trip. While I was gone, he was sick and couldn't go to daycare, so Steve's aunt had taken care of Keegan. It was getting harder and harder to leave him since I was traveling so much with work. As Douglas spoke those words, I knew it was time to be a stay-at-home mom.

Steve and I had talked on and off about me staying home. As he liked to remind me, his name was on the building he walked into and mine was not on the building I walked into. So, the next day I went into Douglas and handed him my resignation. It was bittersweet.

GARNSEY ROAD
BLUEBERRY
CHEESECAKE

BLUEBERRY
MOJITOS

BLUEBERRY
MARGARITA

Garnsey Road Blueberry Cheesecake

Serves 6

Crust:

24 crushed graham crackers or 1 ¼ cup already crushed
½ cup sugar
4 tablespoons unsalted butter, cut into bits and softened
¼ cup cinnamon

In a food processor, process the graham crackers until they form fine crumbs. Add sugar, butter and cinnamon, process until it is well mixed. Put the crumb mixture in a Springform pan. Pat the mixture onto bottom of pan and halfway up the sides. Refrigerate until firm.

Filling:

4 eggs
1 cup sugar
1½ lbs cream cheese at room temperature
2 tablespoons fresh lemon juice
1 teaspoon pure vanilla extract
¾ pint of fresh blueberries

Preheat oven to 375°

With a mixer, beat ingredients one at a time in the order given, beating briefly after each addition. Once everything is added, beat for about 15-20 minutes. Fold in fresh blueberries, and pour the filling into the crust and spread until smooth. Bake the cheesecake in the middle of the oven for about 50 minutes. Take out and let cake stand for about 10 minutes. Change the oven temperature to 475° and let preheat while making the topping.

Topping:
1 cup sour cream
2 tablespoons sugar
½ teaspoon pure vanilla extract
Pinch of kosher salt
Blueberry Haven Blueberry Topping

Mix together all topping ingredients and cover top of cake
with mixture. Return cake to oven and bake 5 minutes.
Remove from oven and top with Blueberry Haven Blueberry
Topping and sprinkle with fresh blueberries. Garnish with
mint sprigs, if desired.

Blueberry Mojitos

Serves 3

30 Mint leaves
A handful of blueberries
6 oz of your favorite rum
6 oz Blueberry Haven Blueberry Elixir
6 tablespoons of freshly squeezed lime juice (about 3 limes)
Soda water

Muddle the mint leaves and lime juice with a mortar and
pestle. Put into a large pitcher and add the rum, elixir, and
soda water to taste. Stir. Pour over ice and garnish with
mint and a couple of fresh blueberries floating on top

Blueberry Margarita

Serves 3

Ice
Fresh blueberries
6 oz Blueberry Haven Blueberry Elixir
6 oz tequila
3 oz lime juice
Lime wedge
Coarse salt

Combine ice, Blueberry Haven Blueberry Elixir, lime juice
and tequila in a boston shaker and shake well. Rub rim of
glasses with lime wedge and dip in salt. Divide the
margarita mixture between the prepared glasses and serve.
Garnish with fresh blueberries and lime.

We Should Buy That Cottage

Steve and I were still living in Grand Rapids in 1995, the year Keegan was born, and we (really I) had been looking for a new house. The public elementary school where our current house was located was not a school I wanted Keegan to attend, so I was looking for other areas and houses.

Steve and I were having a hard time agreeing where to look, so we looked mostly in the Forest Hills School district. The summer and fall before, we had spent a lot of time at the beaches in the Grand Haven and Holland area. We had looked at a couple cottages in Holland and West Olive, as well. At the end of January, right before Keegan's first birthday and about two weeks before I resigned, I thought I had found the perfect house in the Forest Hills Northern School district. I called the realtor, and we looked at the house for the third time. It was a new home with large closets, a big kitchen and family room all attached. After the realtor dropped us off at our house, we got Keegan to bed and started talking.

"I think we should buy that cottage we looked at this fall in West Olive," Steve said.

"You're kidding me, right?" I said. But I was really thinking, *I have spent more time with a realtor in the past two weeks, and you think we should buy a cottage that is really no more than a glorified garage in West Olive?*

In September of 1995, we had looked at a little cement block cottage built in 1949 that was overpriced. However, it sat right on the shores of Lake Michigan and the beach was only steps from the front door. The property had been a nursery at one time, so there was a long driveway off Lakeshore Drive to the house. I was still thinking he was pulling my leg.

"That cottage has been for sale for a long time. Obviously there is a reason it's not selling," Steve said.

"Did you see the bathroom in that place? My outhouse bathroom on Cold Stream was better than that," I said.

During the sale process, we discovered that the lady who owned the house was four years behind in the taxes, needed the cash and lived in the St. Louis area. The cottage had been built by her parents, and they had spent all her summers there while she grew up in the Grand Rapids area. Her father had been a local pharmacist.

It was 1996, I had quit my job, Keegan turned one, and we put an offer in on the cottage. I think Steve convinced me I would love living in Grand Haven for summers, and that Keegan, Sawyer and I could spend every day at the beach. We would also have our own place to go in the summer, and we wouldn't always be camping out at our parents' houses.

We took possession in what would become our little slice of heaven in West Olive in April of 1996, and we moved out to the cottage for the summer by Memorial Day. We did a few little things to the cottage but mostly just spruced it up with some bright colored furniture, pillows and fabrics. It was tiny, with just one bathroom that had a shower stall and sink. Keegan loved taking his baths in the kitchen sink. It had two bedrooms, a great room with eating area, and a screened-in porch off the back where we put another bed and called it the sleeping porch. The cottage had wooden floors throughout that were very rustic, so Keegan's cars could run everywhere in the house, and if Sawyer was wet and sandy, who cared? It was the cottage.

While Steve worked, Keegan, Sawyer and I spent our days on the beach and in the water. My Gantos friend, Laura, came out a lot with her kids to the beach and taught me to make jam. We made raspberry, strawberry and blueberry jam, and I was hooked on homemade jam.

I made a ton in the summer, so I could have it all year long to give to friends and families for gifts throughout the year.

Keegan spent a lot of time running between our cottage and the cottage to the south of us, where a widowed lady named DJ (Dorothy Jane) Kliner lived. Her parents had bought the property from the people who had originally owned our cottage, and she was very concerned about who her neighbors were going to be, because they lived close enough to pass the salt through the window. DJ took me and Keegan under her wing and showed us everything our new cottage had to offer. She also took us to the best spots to pick blueberries, driving us to her favorite farm and helping Keegan fill his bucket as full as he could. DJ loved to watch Keegan on the beach, because he had blonde hair and blue eyes like her grandson who was of Dutch heritage. She would laugh when she saw Keegan running so fast down the beach and comment on how he "looked just like a sand piper running down the beach." DJ taught us the history of our little cottage and the surrounding area. She filled us in on who owned the cottages right down the beach from us, and even showed us the cottage that is featured in the American Pie movie -- it was only six houses away from our cottage.

DJ also told us about how the Tom Hanks' movie, the Road to Perdition, was filmed that summer on the shores of Lake Michigan, just a mile to the south. We continuously stretched our summers to be as long as we could, which meant staying at the cottage with no heat. So, we often had to head back to our home in Grand Rapids by the end of September.

On DJ's birthday, April 6th, 1998, our second son, James Campbell Balk, was born and DJ was elated. We also had new neighbors move into the north of us who were from the Grand Rapids area as well. Again, this family (the Hoekmans) also became like framily to us. DJ and Ma Hoek have given me many fantastic recipes, as has DJ's daughter Nancy, who inherited DJ's cottage.

Our third son, Cayce (pronounced CASE), was born in January of 2001. He's not Case because of the tractors; he's Cayce because of a cute, little couple with that last name, who were recognized at our church of Westminster Presbyterian. DJ's sister Maw Maw had three boys, and she came every summer and was at home with all of my boys. By this time, we had outgrown our house and the two bedroom cottage. Again we looked in Forest Hills for a new house, and I found what I thought was the perfect house.

"I think we should move to the lake," Steve said.

So we constructed a new home on the property where the little cottage had stood. We saved as many artifacts as we could from the cottage -- the doors that connected the house to the screened in porch and a lot of the original white pine floor that is in Steve's office and Campbell's bedroom today. We moved into our home in West Olive in Grand Haven Township full time in the summer of 2001. For kindergarten, we had put Keegan in St. Andrews, a Catholic school, in downtown Grand Rapids, but he started first grade at Rosy Mound in Grand Haven Public Schools.

CHICKEN CURRY with
BLUEBERRIES and
DRIED BLUEBERRY
BASMATI RICE

BLUEBERRY CRISP

Chicken Curry with Blueberries and Dried Blueberry Basmati Rice

Serves 4

Curry:
¾ tablespoon of coriander (finely chopped)
1 cup of blueberries (fresh or frozen)
2 tablespoons of grated ginger
1¼ cup of low-fat Greek yogurt
4 cloves of garlic, chopped
3 tablespoons olive oil
1 teaspoon turmeric
2 tablespoons ground cinnamon
1 teaspoon chili powder
4 chicken breasts, chopped
1 teaspoon Garam Masala
Salt to taste

In a small bowl, blend together coriander, blueberries, ginger and the low-fat Greek yogurt. Set aside. In a sauté pan, add olive oil and garlic and cook until brown; add turmeric, cinnamon and chili powder and stir for about 20 seconds. Add the chicken pieces and stir; pour in yogurt mixture and simmer for 10 minutes or until chicken is cooked, stirring occasionally. Add the Garam Masala.

Rice:
2 teaspoons cumin seeds
2 tablespoons olive oil
1 small onion, chopped
1 teaspoon turmeric
1 carrot, grated
1 cup Basmati rice
½ cup Blueberry Haven Dried Blueberries
Salt to taste

In a small pan, add olive oil and cumin seeds, cook 2-3 minutes until the seeds pop. Add onion, turmeric, grated carrot, and cook for about two minutes. Add this mixture to the uncooked Basmati rice, along with a little salt and 1-2 cups of boiling water. Cook for 4 minutes. Stir and cook another 3-4 minutes. Cover the pan and cook for another 3-4 minutes. After it is cooked, add the Blueberry Haven Dried Blueberries and let stand for a 7-10 minutes before serving.

Blueberry Crisp

Serves 4

3 cups of blueberries

Preheat oven to 400°

In an 8"x8" glass pan (sprayed with cooking oil), layer the blueberries and bake for 10 minutes.

Topping:
¼ cup brown sugar
½ cup oatmeal
1 tablespoons butter
1 tablespoons flour

Mix together brown sugar, oatmeal, butter and flour in a bowl. Crumble mixture over the blueberries and bake for 10 minutes. Reduce heat to 350° and cook for 25 additional minutes.

Our House on the Big Lake

We loved our new house on the lake and living in Grand Haven. We had plenty of room for the boys and the dog, and spent a lot of time at the

beach. So we were very happy when September came and we didn't have to leave the lake. Keegan was in first grade and Campbell was going to preschool. Cayce and I stayed at home while the boys were at school.

Keegan wanted to play soccer like he had in Grand Rapids, so he got involved in that and soon he was playing travel soccer. To add to all that fun, our friends Paula and Scott had moved back from New Jersey to Ann Arbor and happened to be coming to Holland one fall as their son Zach was playing hockey. We thought it would be fun to go watch Zach play hockey. Soccer had just finished for the season and our boys thought hockey looked like fun. What did I know? I was never a hockey mom, just a hockey girlfriend. We let the boys learn to skate and before long all three were playing hockey. Just as quickly, they went from playing house hockey to travel hockey. With all three of them playing travel hockey, it basically meant we drove all over the mitten every weekend.

It was nuts -- we met nutty people and our kids played for nutty coaches. Pretty soon we were nutty just like all the nutty hockey people; however, deep down we loved the game as much as our kids.

Our house was often what we called the hockey rotation. Either the boys were in the playroom with mini sticks, in the driveway shooting, skating at the blueberry fields that were frozen over, or at the rink. Our summer vacations usually revolved around where the boys went to hockey camp. The first camp they went to was at the University of Maine. We stayed at Cold Stream and drove the boys to camp every day. One of the counselors, Jimmy Howard, had recently been drafted by the Red Wings, and Keegan was even lucky enough to get to shoot on him. They only let two kids shoot on Jimmy all camp, and it was the "kid from Michigan" and a boy from Massachusetts. That was the first trip the boys took to Cold Stream.

The number Keegan picked to be his own number was 25, because two and five were his Grandpa's lucky numbers. Campbell chose to be number 52, and because 25 plus 52 equaled 77, Cayce chose to be number 77.

In the summer of 2007, Keegan and Campbell went to a hockey camp in Sudbury, Ontario. It was more like a true summer camp on a lake where they swam, fished and stayed in cabins. However, the camp director was a  retired New Jersey NHL player, and every afternoon they skated at the local rink. By then we had a 6-month-old Chesapeake Bay Retriever puppy named Bruin, named after the Boston Bruins. Bruin was also a Canadian Chessie. One of our hockey coach's parents had raised Chessies for years, and his Blue Ribbon Chessie had just sired his first litter. Sawyer, our first Chessie, had passed away a few years back. When Sawyer was 10, we got Cally, also a Chesapeake Bay Retriever, short for

Calgary -- the Calgary Flames. We had hoped that Sawyer would help train Cally, but Cally, now 4, was still not very well trained. We say she's pretty but not very smart. So here we were with two big, brown smelly dogs -- Bruin and Cally.

We rented a little cottage from the camp directors, which was located next to their home. While the boys were away at camp, we lounged at the lake and in the sauna, went for speed boat rides, and Cayce fished right off the dock. We had a very relaxing time and were grateful to our hosts, who were very generous to us during our stay at their cottage. Like many years before, we were driving home with all the hockey gear in the way back of the black Suburban, Cayce and Bruin in the third row, Keegan and Campbell in the bucket seats, and Steve and I up front. As we were nearing our home, Steve and I were discussing what we could send to the Crowders who had been so generous to us. We were on Lake Michigan Drive, almost to US 31, amongst acres and acres of blueberry fields, and Steve says, "How about something from Cherry Republic?"

"We really need a Blueberry Re...haven," I said. It was then that the wheels in my head really started turning.

BAKED BLUEBERRY
FRENCH TOAST

HOMEMADE
BLUEBERRY GRANOLA

Baked Blueberry French Toast

Serves 4

4 eggs
2 egg yolks
1 cup milk
1 cup whipping cream
2 tablespoons sugar
1½ teaspoons vanilla
2 cups blueberries
½ cup of butter
¼ cup packed brown sugar
¾ teaspoon cinnamon
French baguette, cut diagonally into 1/2-inch thick slices
Powdered sugar, to sprinkle on top.

Preheat oven to 350°

Melt one stick of butter in 13" x 9" glass pan; once melted, sprinkle the brown sugar onto the melted butter. In a large bowl, whisk eggs, milk, cream, sugar and vanilla; dip the bread in the mixture until well coated. Place bread slices in pan and sprinkle with blueberries. Bake at 350° until puffed and blueberries pop, 55-60 minutes. Sprinkle powdered sugar on top right as the pan comes out of the oven.

Homemade Blueberry Granola

Serves 4

3 cups old-fashioned oats
2 cups unsweetened coconut chips
1 cup Blueberry Haven Dried Blueberries
½ cup coarsely chopped raw pecans
¼ cup brown sugar
3 tablespoons canola oil
3 tablespoons Blueberry Haven Blossom Honey
1 teaspoon pure vanilla extract
Fresh blueberries, for serving

Preheat oven to 325°

Toss the oats, coconut chips, blueberries and pecans in a large bowl. In a small bowl, whisk together the brown sugar, canola oil, honey and vanilla, and drizzle over the oat mixture. Stir well so everything is evenly coated. Use your hands to toss and make sure every piece of oat is covered. Spread the mixture in an even layer on a rimmed baking sheet. Bake until golden brown in the center of the oven, 15 minutes, rotating the baking sheet halfway through baking and stirring the granola with a spoon so it will cook evenly. Remove from the oven and add to a large bowl so it will stop cooking. Let cool before serving.

We Need a Blueberry Haven

The rest of the summer of 2007, I traveled to stores and farmers markets and picked my friends' brains about Blueberry Haven. There was a store with all things blueberry in a town to the South, but it was nothing like my idea for Blueberry Haven. A great little bake shop had opened in Grand Haven in 2005, and I had been their first customer and frequented their cafe often. I spoke to them about my idea to see if they would be willing to help me find a way to package all my great recipes. Not only could they help me, but also they could make my recipes even better and add their special twist on Blueberry Haven. Elegance of the Seasons' Julie and Michelle were perfect business women, a great mother-daughter team, my friends and my design team.

We also had a family friend who was in the commercial loan business, and I asked for his advice.

"It's a great idea, and if you don't do it, I'm going to," he said.

I don't think he really would have, but I think he knew that would give me a kick in the butt. I refer to his son as my fourth son, as I often think I should have that child's social security number and claim him on our taxes. He walks in the house and says "Hi, Mom," and checks to see what we are having for dinner.

I had some other very good friends who were instrumental in guiding me as I began my adventure. One was a husband and wife -- she is a marketing project manager and he is a systems guru. Cayce's godmother, Kathy, a former colleague at Gantos and a whiz at stock planning, continuously cheered me on and helped me move forward. The boys and Steve were patient and helpful as I became consumed with the idea of opening Blueberry Haven. I vowed that I would not let this project keep me away from my mom and wife duties, and I would not let work become my top priority. So if this happened, it would happen as time, family and life permitted.

In September of 2007, Cayce was entering first grade, and at seven, he would be going to school all day. Campbell was in fourth grade, and Keegan was in seventh grade. All three boys were playing travel hockey on teams out of Grand Rapids, while we still lived on the lake in Grand Haven, with Cally and Bruin.

On September 7th, 2007, my little #77 and I filed the LLC for Blueberry Haven. Filing the LLC was all legal mumbo jumbo, and I had nothing but ideas and product in the works -- concepts but nothing concrete. I took my ideas and packaging to Dave, the owner of Holland Wooden Bowl Company in Holland. I was interested in gift bowls to go with my idea and wanted everything to be made in Michigan.

"Honey, this is a great idea, and I want you to meet my friend Diana. She has a store in downtown Holland and has a Michigan food pantry," Dave said. "You need to meet her."

I went down the street to The Shaker Messenger in Holland and met with Diana. I did not have products yet, only prototypes of what the product would look like. At this time it was the beginning of November and Christmas was right around the corner. Diana looked at all my products and said that as soon as I had stock, she would take a dozen of everything. I walked out of her store and could NOT believe my luck.

The first week in December, I delivered Blueberry Jam, Pancake Mix, Blue Chocolate Covered Blueberries, and Dried Blueberries to Diana. That was my entire product line. I had a reorder within a week and double the quantity. In retail, those sell through rates and reorders are basically unheard of, and it has been that way ever since.

This was just the beginning of many doors that would open for Blueberry Haven. I continued to land stores to carry my product -- Fortino's in Grand Haven, The Butler Pantry in Saugatuck and the Art of the Table in Grand Rapids. There were a few other stores that we tried, however, we felt the products were not selling quickly enough at those stores, so we decided to stay with the four initial stores.

Next we began attending gift shows throughout the state, as well as selling at the Farmer's Market in Grand Haven. I had initially contacted the gift shows to try to get a foot in the door and get the product known out in the area. After a short time, though, I had stores and gift shows calling us, and we were loyal to those who helped us get started and took a risk on Blueberry Haven. We are now at a point where we currently are not accepting wholesale orders, and we rarely go on the road with Blueberry Haven.

In the winter of 2010, Laura met me for lunch and we went to Elegance of the Seasons. Laura was working for a big shoe company in the Grand Rapids area with Cayce's godmother, Kathy. While we were eating lunch, we were brainstorming. I told Laura that I really thought I needed a storefront to get people to understand what Blueberry Haven was, since many in West Michigan didn't travel north and had never heard of American Spoon or Cherry Republic.   Laura and I were chatting away at lunch when we looked up at the same time and saw the empty building across the street with a sign in the window that said, For rent.

"What about that place?" Laura said.

"Steve won't want to rent," I said, but I wrote down the number, and later that night I handed Steve the phone number.

TIFFANY'S
HOCKEY MOM CHICKEN

SWEET POTATO CHIPS

BLUEBERRY CHOCOLATE
POUND CAKE with
CHOCOLATE BUTTER
CREAM FROSTING

Tiffany's
Hockey Mom Chicken

Serves 4

4 chicken breasts (boneless and skinless)
1 Jar Blueberry Haven Blueberry Barbecue Sauce

Place chicken breasts and barbecue sauce in crock pot.
Cook on low all day. It will shred as you pull it out of the
crock pot. Serve on your favorite bun as a barbecue chicken
sandwich.

Sweet Potato Chips

Serves 6

3 large sweet potatoes (this will make about 3 cookie sheets
worth of chips, or about 6 servings)
Cracked sea salt and pepper, M-Salt
Cooking spray oil (I like Pam with Olive Oil)
Seasonings

Preheat oven to 450°

Slice the sweet potatoes into very thin (⅛ inch or less)
slices. If you have a mandolin, use it because you want them
all to be the same thickness so they will cook evenly. Line
cookie sheets with aluminum foil and spray with oil. Place
sweet potato slices on cookie sheets, so none are on top of
each other. Spray with more oil, and sprinkle with generous
amounts of sea salt, pepper and M-Salt. Bake for 15-20
minutes.

Blueberry Chocolate Pound Cake with
Chocolate Butter Cream Frosting

Serves 6

3 sticks margarine or butter

3 teaspoons vanilla

3 cups sugar

½ cup cocoa

5 eggs

½ teaspoon baking powder

3 cups all purpose flour

1 cup milk (preferably whole milk)

1 cup Blueberry Haven Jam, any flavor

Preheat oven to 325°

Grease and flour Bundt pan and set aside. Cream butter in large mixing bowl. Add sugar, and beat until light and fluffy. Add eggs, one at a time, beating well after each addition. In a separate bowl, stir together flour, cocoa and baking powder. Measure milk and stir vanilla into it. Add wet ingredients and dry ingredients alternately, mixing after each addition. Fold the jam into the cake batter for a fruity swirl.

Pour into pan and bake for one hour and twenty minutes. Let cool for ten minutes before removing from pan and allowing to cool completely before frosting.

Butter Cream Frosting

1 pound bittersweet chocolate
12 ounces semisweet chocolate
¾ cup egg whites (4 to 5 extra-large eggs), at room temperature
1½ cups granulated sugar
¼ teaspoon cream of tartar
¾ teaspoon kosher salt
1½ pounds unsalted butter, at room temperature
3 teaspoons pure vanilla extract
3 teaspoons instant espresso powder, dissolved in 1½ teaspoons water
3 tablespoons dark rum, if desired

Chop the chocolates and place them in a double boiler. Stir until melted, then set aside until cooled to room temperature.

Mix the egg whites, sugar, cream of tartar and salt in the bowl of an electric mixer fitted with a whisk attachment. Place the bowl of egg whites over the pan of simmering water and heat the egg whites until they are warm to the touch, about 5 minutes. Return the bowl to the electric mixer and whisk on high speed for 5 minutes, or until the meringue is cool and holds a stiff peak. Add the butter, 1 tablespoon at a time, while beating on medium speed. Scrape down the bowl and add the melted chocolate, vanilla, espresso, and rum (if using), and mix for 1 minute or until the chocolate is completely blended in. If the buttercream seems very soft, allow it to cool, and beat it again.

Blueberry Haven Opens Its Doors

Steve called the real estate agent and asked if they would be willing to sell and not rent. They agreed, and In December of 2010, we closed on the storefront. Blueberry Haven now had a brick and mortar building at 213 Washington in downtown Grand Haven. The building had been home to many different businesses over the years and was a great structure of a building. Inside it was dark, dreary and just blah. I went to work drawing exactly what I wanted the store to look like -- the shelves, flooring, walls and ceilings. I took ideas from different stores throughout the United States for the store design. It is a cross between L.L. Bean and Stonewall Kitchen, meets Kate Spade at the beach in Grand Haven, and opens a Blueberry Boutique. Just like our tagline Beaches, Berries and Bliss.

We hired a local contractor to help with our vision and needed an architect to seal the deal. Everything in the store was picked out and designed by me. I had pictures of every aspect, and showed the carpenter exact replicas of the check-out desk and shelves, even though I had seen them in a different material in other stores. I wanted an open ceiling, and I wanted everything to be the blueberry blue color of my labels. It looked great, and even the painter (who looked like an Oompa Loompa when he was done), thought it was fantastic. When I went to the lighting store, I didn't know what I wanted, yet I knew what I didn't want. My brother-in-law had helped with the lighting design, and he sent me to a fantastic lighting store in Grand Rapids. I told the saleswoman I wanted something crystal and chandelier-like but with a modern take. She had just the perfect suggestion and we have received numerous compliments on the lights in our store.

We were hoping we would be open by Memorial Day of 2011, but had a few delays working with the city. I wanted a couple of specialty items (like my drinking fountains) that were different from other stores in Grand Haven. That held us up. The architect and the contractor held us up a little as well.

Finally, on November 11, 2011 (11-11-11), it was ready to go, and we opened the doors with a soft opening, no grand opening. Of course, we knew it was not a coincidental date, as it was the hockey number of that fourth son of mine.

From the start of Blueberry Haven, one door after another has opened and one connection has lead to another and another. Be it my family, friends, or friends of friends and family, the crazy number connections have a significance, and I am still listening to what the next plans are for Blueberry Haven. We are continuously adding products and have come a long way since our first four products of Blue Chocolate Covered Blueberries, Blueberry Jam, Dried Blueberries, and the Cinna-berry Pancake Mix. Now we have six types of blueberry jams, condiments, chocolates, six dry mixes, coffees and much, much more as we continue to develop more products.

Whether it is the people we are working with, the people who walk in the door at Blueberry Haven, or someone I've known previously or have had a connection with, Blueberry Haven keeps evolving. Everything is made in Michigan and most everything is made right in Grand Haven from the fruit of our town.

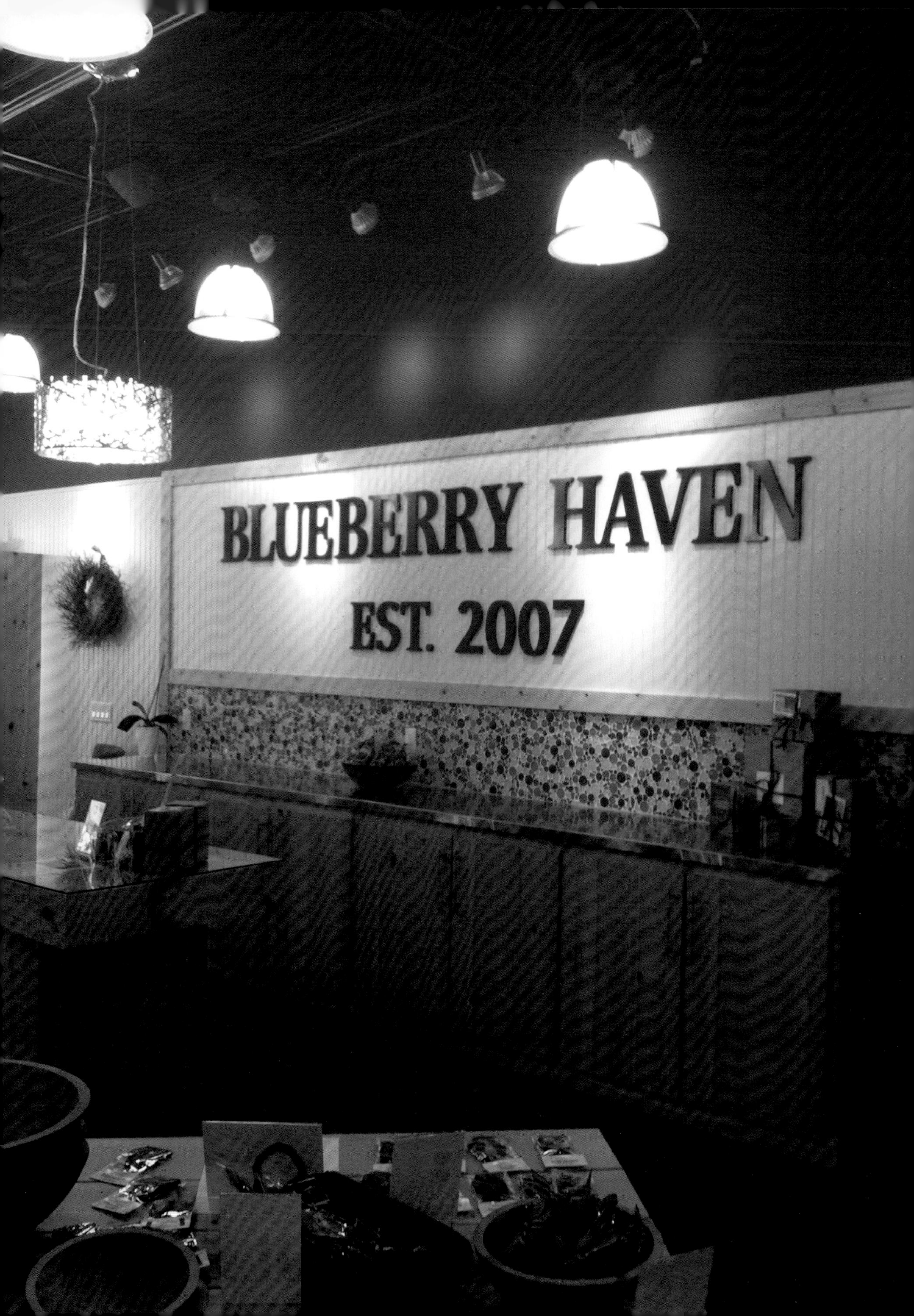
BLUEBERRY HAVEN
EST. 2007

HONEY GLAZED CARROTS
with PEARLIZED ONIONS
AND MINT

FILET MIGNON with
BLUEBERRY BOURBON
SAUCE

THE COAST GUARD CAKE

Honey Glazed Carrots with Pearlized Onions and Mint

Serves 4

1 lb carrots
½ lb pearl onions
3 tablespoons butter
3 tablespoons Blueberry Haven Blossom Honey
1½ tablespoons fresh lemon juice
Sea salt
Ground pepper
1/3 cup fresh mint

In a skillet, bring 2/3 cups water to a boil; add salt, carrots and onions, and cook until tender. Drain water. Add Blueberry Haven Blossom Honey and lemon juice, and cook until a glaze forms, about 5 minutes. Season with salt and pepper, and toss with the mint leaves.

Filet Mignon with Blueberry Bourbon Sauce

Serves 4

Bourbon Sauce:
1½ teaspoons olive oil
½ chopped small red onion
2 chopped garlic cloves
1 jalapeño pepper, seeded and chopped
¼ cup bourbon
1 cup fresh blueberries
¼ cup ketchup
3 tablespoons cider vinegar
1 tablespoon brown sugar
Pinch of allspice

Heat oil in saucepan over medium heat. Add onion and cook until tender and starting to brown. Add garlic and jalapeño, and cook about 30 seconds. Add bourbon, increase heat and bring to boil; cook until most of the liquid is gone, about 2-5 minutes. Stir in blueberries, ketchup, vinegar, brown sugar and allspice, and return to boil. Reduce heat and simmer, stirring until thickened, 15-20 minutes.

For Filet:
1 tablespoon chopped fresh thyme
1 tablespoon olive oil
¾ teaspoon salt
½ teaspoon ground pepper
4 - 4 oz filet mignons

Preheat grill to high. Mix thyme, oil, salt and pepper in a small bowl. Rub mixture on all sides of steak. Grill steaks 3-5 minutes per side for medium rare. Let rest 5 minutes before serving with the sauce.

The Coast Guard Cake

Serves 6

3 cups flour
1 tablespoon baking powder
½ teaspoon salt
1 cup buttermilk
2 teaspoons grated lemon zest
1½ teaspoon vanilla
1 cup unsalted butter at room temperature
2 cups sugar
3 large eggs
2 large egg yolks

Preheat oven to 350°

Grease bottoms and sides of 2 (9-inch) round cake pans. Line bottom of pans with parchment paper; grease and flour, and tap out excess flour.

In large bowl, mix together flour, baking powder and salt. Set aside. In small bowl, mix buttermilk, lemon zest and vanilla. Set aside. Beat butter and sugar together in another bowl; on medium speed until light and fluffy. Add eggs and then yolks, one at a time. Mix on low speed, and then add flour mixture and buttermilk mixture, alternately, starting and ending with the flour mixture. Mix until combined.

Pour batter into cake pans and bake about 35 minutes or until lightly golden brown. Test the center with a toothpick to make sure it is cooked. Cool at least 10 minutes before turning upside down and taking out the parchment paper on the bottom.

Filling:
3 cups blueberries
1 tablespoon lemon juice
1/3 cup granulated sugar
1½ teaspoons lemon zest
2 tablespoons water
5 teaspoons cornstarch

In a medium sauce pan, boil blueberries, lemon juice, sugar and lemon zest. Reduce to a simmer and cook about 15 minutes or until blueberries have popped and sauce thickens. Combine water and cornstarch in a small cup. Pour cornstarch mixture into blueberry mixture and return to a boil. Boil about 1 minute, stirring constantly. Let cool.

If you don't have time to make filling you can use 2 jars of Blueberry Haven Blueberry Topping instead.

Frosting:
12 oz cream cheese at room temperature
10 tablespoons unsalted butter at room temperature
1 teaspoon vanilla
2½ cups powdered sugar

Beat cream cheese, butter and vanilla with mixer on medium high speed until blended. Add sugar and mix on low speed until mixed together.

After frosting cake, top with about 2 cups of fresh blueberries and 1 cup of fresh strawberries.

Blueberry Haven Ingredients

B

Barbecue Sauce, *248*

Blueberry Topping, *86, 199, 209, 217, 265*

C

Chutney, *110, 140, 158, 172, 180*

D

Dried Blueberries, *26, 34, 54, 97, 106, 121, 125, 158, 228, 241*

E

Elixir, *46, 195, 219, 220*

G

Ground Blueberry Coffee, *37*

H

Honey, *29, 65, 99, 106, 167, 241, 260*

Honey Mustard, *74, 94, 118, 168*

J

Jam, *44, 53, 66, 77, 109, 252*

S

Salsa, *140*

Recipe Index

Tiffany's Hockey Mom Chicken, *248*

Turkey Sliders with Blueberry
Ketchup, *74*

W

White Chocolate Tart with
Blueberries, *187*

White Fish Tacos, *140*

Meal Planning Index

White Chocolate Tart with Blueberries, 187

Main Course

Baked Salmon with Blueberry Sauce, 196

Chicken Curry with Blueberries and Dried Blueberry Basmati Rice, 228

Chicken Satay with Blueberry Sauce, 109

Crispy Blueberry Haven Mustard Chicken, 94

Filet Mignon with Blueberry Bourbon Sauce, 263

Grilled Blueberry Pork Tenderloins, 180

Lamb Chops with Blueberry Relish, 206

Roasted Chicken with Blueberry Peppercorn Sauce, 118

Salmon and Blueberry Cherry Tomato Crostini, 168

Steamed Clams, 85

Steamed Lobsters, 83

Tiffany's Hockey Mom Chicken, 248

Turkey Sliders with Blueberry Ketchup, 74

White Fish Tacos, 140

Salads

Blueberry Quinoa Salad with Lemon Basil Dressing, 54

Chicken Blueberry Chutney Salad, 158

Lobster Salad with Blueberries, 19

Michigan Blue Cheese Blueberry Salad, 97

Sides

Blueberry Biscuits, 99

Blueberry Cornbread Stuffing, 121

Blueberry Ketchup, 74

Blueberry Jalapeno Cornbread, 161

Blueberry Peppercorn Sauce, 118

Blueberry Vinaigrette, 98

Brussel Sprouts, 122

Honey Glazed Carrots with Pearlized Onions and Mint, 260

Roasted Asparagus, 184

Shirley's Mashed Potatoes, 183

Sweet Potato Chips, 251